About Island Press

Since 1984, the nonprofit organization Island Press has been stimulating, shaping, and communicating ideas that are essential for solving environmental problems worldwide. With more than 1,000 titles in print and some 30 new releases each year, we are the nation's leading publisher on environmental issues. We identify innovative thinkers and emerging trends in the environmental field. We work with world-renowned experts and authors to develop cross-disciplinary solutions to environmental challenges.

Island Press designs and executes educational campaigns, in conjunction with our authors, to communicate their critical messages in print, in person, and online using the latest technologies, innovative programs, and the media. Our goal is to reach targeted audiences—scientists, policy makers, environmental advocates, urban planners, the media, and concerned citizens—with information that can be used to create the framework for long-term ecological health and human well-being.

Island Press gratefully acknowledges major support from The Bobolink Foundation, Caldera Foundation, The Curtis and Edith Munson Foundation, The Forrest C. and Frances H. Lattner Foundation, The JPB Foundation, The Kresge Foundation, The Summit Charitable Foundation, Inc., and many other generous organizations and individuals.

The opinions expressed in this book are those of the author(s) and do not necessarily reflect the views of our supporters.

Meet Me at the Library

Meet Me at the Library

A Place to Foster
Social Connection and
Promote Democracy

Shamichael Hallman

ISLANDPRESS | Washington | Covelo

Library of Congress Control Number: 2024938234

All Island Press books are printed on environmentally responsible materials.

Manufactured in the United States of America
10 9 8 7 6 5 4 3 2 1

Keywords: belonging, bridging activities, civic health, civic infrastructure, civic renewal, community event, community participation, Cossitt Library, digital divide, digital equity, inclusion, librarian, Library of Things, library services, loneliness, Memphis Public Library, partnership, public library, public participation, social infrastructure, volunteer, workforce development

To librarians and library professionals across the globe.

Contents

Foreword: To Garden Our Democracy

by Eric Liu

A COMMUNITY IS NOT A MACHINE. It is not a cogs-and-gears device or an elegant algorithm designed by an engineer to maximize efficiency. A community is a garden: a complex adaptive ecosystem in which all kinds of life is striving to thrive, a riot of diversity with the potential for both beautiful bounty and terrible chaos. Left to itself, a garden will eventually be overrun by weeds. Gardens require gardeners.

There are no better gardeners of our democracy than public librarians. A librarian knows how to seed and feed the civic imagination. A librarian knows how to invite many hands into the work of cultivation for the good of all. A librarian can see when something noxious is taking root in a young person's mind and tend to it. A librarian can turn strangers into friends who then turn separate ideas into hybrids. A librarian can introduce us to the tools we need to govern ourselves—knowledge of our past, skills for the present, curiosity about the future.

Shamichael Hallman is a master civic gardener, and this powerful book is not just a chronicle of his professional and personal commitment to the library but also a praise song for local democracy and a picture of what is possible when we commit to democracy—even when we have many reasons to walk away from it.

I lead a national nonprofit organization called Citizen University that is working to build a culture of powerful, responsible citizenship all across the United States. I have not known a civic catalyst more powerful than Shamichael. We first met when he was the manager of the Cossitt Library in Memphis, a branch of that city's public library system with an honored place in that city's Black history and a vital role in the making of a new civic commons along the riverfront. He embodied the history and the future alike with an open-minded, open-hearted, can-do communal spirit captured in the title of this book.

Meet Me at the Library

I did meet Shamichael at the library, and in many other places in Memphis and around the country. He hosted a program called CitizenFEST that combined barbecue, the blues, and joyful civic lessons in local power. He invited people who had never been invited to claim their city this way. He later became one of the first people we trained to lead Civic Saturdays, a civic analogue to a faith gathering, and he led these gatherings right in the middle of the Cossitt Library in the middle of the day to attract the passersby and patrons who didn't know they needed a ritual like this, a space to make sense of the changing times in their community. Soon he was leading Civic Saturdays in branches across the city. And then he joined the Civic Collaboratory, a nationwide mutual-aid network that my organization runs, and he became one of its most prolific makers of commitments of help to other civic innovators from around the country.

From the very local to the very national and beyond, from the Cossitt Library to a Loeb Fellowship at Harvard to his pacesetting work now at the Urban Libraries Council, Shamichael has amassed a storehouse of practical learnings and teachings and relatable stories of impact that he is now circulating with you.

How to create a feeling of invitation and welcome across the lines that divide us. How to be an ambassador—for your line of work, your community, the unheard and uninvited. How to organize networks of collaborators from many sectors and activate among them a sense of common purpose. How to change the narrative of what your institution is, and is for. How to cultivate what we call at Citizen University "bonds of trust and affection." How to promote a sense of possibility without being a self-promoter. How to serve, live, love, learn, listen, speak, and build like a citizen.

And yes, in this time when libraries and library professionals are under rhetorical and actual assault for trying to keep minds open and books on shelves, Shamichael, who knows with equal compassion what drives some people to hunger for books and what drives others to want to ban them, has ideas here for how to defend the profession. The institution. The garden of democracy. Democracy itself.

You don't need to be a librarian to apply these insights. You need only to be a member of a community who wants to contribute to it and help create the future you imagine for it. But I will admit, as the son of a former public librarian, as an author and lover of books, and as a former trustee of the Seattle Public Library, that I have special a place in my heart for librarians—and an extra-special place for Shamichael Hallman.

I have come to know him as a colleague, a collaborator, a student, a teacher, and a friend. Now you get to know him, too, and to be inspired by his civic-horticultural gifts. Read this book. Then go forth and garden. Our democracy is depending on us.

Preface

SOME OF MY FONDEST MEMORIES as a teenager involved the public library. I was an introverted, sensitive child, and libraries were among the few places that felt safe to me due to their quiet nature. The local library a few towns over connected me to knowledge and information. The librarians were always nice and able to help me find whatever materials I might need to complete a school project or report. Public libraries offered me a first glance at the outside world. I can vividly remember sitting in the children's section of the library staring at reference books that provided insights about Africa, astronomy, airplanes, and athletes. These were some of my favorite topics to explore. And just as someone in the 2020s might follow a seemingly endless chain of linked articles on a website such as Wikipedia, I would spend countless hours at the local library in 1990s flipping through and cross-referencing the pages of Encyclopedia Britannica—a print encyclopedia that was widely available at that time. Aside from reference materials, a variety of comic books and nonfiction reads were also available. But beyond books, and perhaps more importantly, the local library connected me with other people. Through a variety of after-school and week-end book clubs and activities, the library provided an opportunity for me to meet people who shared similar interests to mine, even though our backgrounds were often totally different. Through the public library I not only learned about the Lockheed SR-71 Black-bird, the works of Maya Angelou, and the Great Pyramid of Giza, I also was introduced to other teens who were fascinated with mil-itary aircraft, wanted to write poetry, and dreamed of their first visit to a foreign land. While the public library provided access to books and information, it also served an equally important role in connecting me to other people whom I might not have otherwise had the opportunity to meet. Little did I know that these experi-ences would play a crucial role in my professional life nearly two decades later.

In the winter of 2016, I was approached by the leadership of the Memphis Public Libraries with the unique opportunity to help give new life to a historic public library branch. It was one of eighteen branches in the library system, and it had an important historical place in the life of the city. Not only was it the first public library erected in Memphis, it played a pivotal role in the quest to make public spaces accessible to Black people during the civil rights era—a history that I would soon learn upon starting my work there. Located in the heart of downtown, which was seeing an uptick in both commercial and residential growth as well as new tourist attractions, this library branch also provided wonder-ful, unobstructed views of the Mississippi River. Yet this was a stagnant branch in need of new ways of reaching a diverse and ever-growing community. It was in need of a fresh vision, one that would situate it among the most innovative public libraries in the country. If renovated properly, this library branch could not only serve as a vital anchor for the community and the entire city—a place where the people of Memphis could learn, create, and share with each other—but also serve as a model for libraries across the nation. The path before me was the work alongside library leadership, staff librarians, community leaders, and national thought leaders. It would become one of the most exciting challenges that I've ever embarked upon.

Up to this point, I'd had no background working in public libraries. My professional path had included a mix of tech and faith in which I'd served as an assistant pastor and chief strategy officer at a multi-site megachurch in Memphis, and as co-leader for a global, faith-inspired weekend hackathon series. Each of these roles involved, through relationship building, understanding people's current reality as compared to a desired future state. The combination of these roles would also go far in equipping me with the skills needed to reimagine a twenty-first-century library that leveraged technology such as augmented reality and artificial intelligence, embed emerging trends such as coworking and the maker movement, and create opportunities for shared experience among people of all incomes and backgrounds.

The task of giving new life to anything is a challenge. Ask anyone who has tried to revive a dying garden, restore a run-down home, or turn around an unprofitable business and they will tell you that the task is not easy. Trying to transform a place such as a library, which serves in many different ways to many different people, is an even greater challenge. Working under a wonderful group of leaders within the Memphis Public Libraries, and alongside an amazing staff, community partners, and passionate residents, we embarked on a multiyear campaign that would ultimately result in a reimagined, award-winning library branch that is now a thriving community anchor. Along the way, I had the wonderful opportunity to visit public libraries across North America. During these trips I spoke with the library leaders and staff who were the driving force behind individual library branches and entire library systems. I saw service models and building designs that challenged my notions of the role that a library could play in its community. I read strategic plans that emphasized the importance of positioning the library as a vital community asset, embracing nontraditional models of achieving community transformation and addressing inequalities, and celebrating the cultural and intellectual vitality of the communities they served. I took copious notes. Each of these visits left me inspired and provided fuel for the work that we were doing in Memphis by helping me understand the importance of intellectual freedom, the enhanced roles that libraries could play if they were designed and funded appropriately, and the unique value proposition of public libraries to create a welcoming space for all. In addition to these experiences, I've also had the pleasure of:

- Launching a grassroots initiative to explore how public libraries of all sizes, and all across the country, were working to foster social cohesion, promote civic renewal, and advance the ideal of a healthy American democracy.
- Giving interviews to international media outlets and delivering lectures and keynotes at universities (the University of South Carolina, Florida International University, Rutgers University, and Princeton University, to name a few) as well as institutions and organizations all over the world about the role of public libraries and democracy.
- Participating in a contemporary study, commissioned by several foundations that sought to identify several core elements of a "community civic infrastructure," and supportive

national resources, that would be necessary to spark, support, and sustain a culture of social cohesion and civic renewal in communities throughout America in the decades to come.

- Visiting countless libraries and other public spaces across the United States in large cities such as Philadelphia, Chicago, and Atlanta, as well as small cities and rural towns such as Rockport, Massachusetts, Eutaw, Alabama, and Edgerton, Kansas.
- Devoting an academic year, as part of the prestigious Loeb Fellowship at the Graduate School of Design at Harvard University, to studying and facilitating dialogue around creating more inclusive, welcoming, and engaging public spaces.

Each of those experiences has provided valuable lessons and a foundation upon which I base the ideas and thoughts behind this book, and you will hear about them in the coming chapters. But beyond informing my professional endeavors, they reignited my personal love for the library and instilled a sense of responsibility not only to help create the next iteration of libraries, but also to tell the story of what I'd seen, through the lens of my personal experiences with public libraries.

I wanted to write this book because I've seen firsthand how libraries are still very much places of learning and community, where all are welcome to expand their horizons. I've witnessed how they are increasing collaboration and problem-solving capacity in their communities. I've observed how they are modeling and creating opportunities for collective impact where institutional and community leaders share and contribute to decision-making. And I'd like to share some of those stories. But I've also seen opportunities where new innovations can arise, especially in light of the current moment in our nation's history. This book is a look at how libraries are shaping and can continue to shape how we see, interact, and think about each other in a society that is increasingly segmented, polarized, and isolating. My hope is that, by reading this book, you will come away with a richer understanding of public libraries as one of the greatest assets our country has—representing a critical civic and social infrastructure that can accomplish great work at the individual and neighborhood level. Libraries are doing the work of stitching communities together. Let's celebrate that fact, and let's work together to ensure that even more of it can happen.

Acknowledgments

I THANK GOD FOR THE WONDERFUL OPPORTUNITY to write this book. It has been an incredible blessing to visit the many locations that influenced it. A journey that started in 2016 has unfolded in ways I could not have imagined. Director Keenon McCloy, Deputy Director Chris Marszalek, and Toni Braswell of the Memphis Public Library not only gave me an opportunity to join their team but trusted me with a momentous task that has helped to transform downtown Memphis. Thankfully, help and support came from a cast of talented staff, including Merlyn Clemmons, Sheila Murphy, Kimberly Boswell, Tina Williams, Colton Morgan, Liz Gilliland, Njeri Robinson, Colton Morgan, Jasmyn Brown, Emily Marks, Ariel Colbert, and Ashia Hardaway. It was a pleasure working with each of them. Due to the work with Memphis Public Library, I was also introduced to the Reimagining the Civic Commons Learning Network and had the great pleasure of connecting with and learning from Bridget Marquis, Carol Coletta, Leslie Carlson, Susan Dalton, and a host of friends across the twelve-city demonstration project.

Few moments have crystallized my life like the opportunity to be trained by the team at Citizen University. I am forever indebted to them, especially its cofounders Eric Liu and Jená Cane. Though her life ended in 2023, Jená's presence is still felt by many.

As my ideas formed around this book's topic, a few like-minded librarians emerged—the chief among them was Daphna Blatt of the New York Public Library. Working together, we found other library professionals who were also passionate about the topic. I would like to specifically acknowledge Annie Tillman, Gypsy Houston, Jenny Garmon, Jennie Garner, Mariah Cherem, Paul Erickson, Timothy Cherubini, and Nancy C. Kranich. Working in collaboration with Darshan Goux and Abhishek Raman of the American Academy of Arts and Sciences, we blazed new trails of understanding about the civic and social impact of public libraries.

I started writing this book during my time as a Loeb Fellow at the Graduate School of Design (GSD) at Harvard University, and a number of people offered guidance and support. A special thanks to my 2023 cohort: Dario Calmese, Pamela Conrad, Claudia Dobles Camargo, Natalia Dopazo, Badruun Gardi, Alberto Kritzler, Rebecca McMackin, and Derwin Sisnett. I would also like to acknowledge a number of faculty and staff at Harvard, including John Peterson, Kweta Henry, Katherine Walker, Anna Lyman, Dean Sara Whiting, Sara Zewde, Diane Davis, Raul Mehrotra, Cory Henry, Danielle Allen, Mina Cikara, Irvin Scott, Raymond Carr, Tracey Hucks, Terrence L. Johnson, Garnette Cadogan, and Elisa Silva, who all took time to share their wisdom over coffee or lunch. Additionally, Alan Ricks and Jha D Amazi's course "The Last Free Space," which focused specifically on public libraries. It offered a number of provocations that provided energy along the way.

Over the last few years, I've met an amazing set of colleagues and new friends who also offered tremendous support during my writing. I would like to acknowledge Carolyn Lukesmyer, Lisa Kay Solomon, Janíce Samuels, Janele Wilson, Pearce Godwin, F. Willis Johnson, Debilyn Moleneux, and the staff at Essential Partners.

Weena Wise helped bring about new understanding of loneliness and social connection, and Cheryl Hughes continually opened doors that changed my life. I am forever grateful to the two of them.

The team at IREX—including Nana Akua Brookman, Phoebe Bierly, Nada Mohamed-Aly, Senior Technical Expert Tara Susman-Peña, and Aisha Thompson-Banton—offered an invitation that changed my life. I hope we continue to do amazing work together!

Each of my colleagues at Urban Libraries Council offered support and encouragement, even though the book was already underway when I joined. A huge thanks to Brooks Rainwater, Director and CEO, for being so supportive.

This book would not be possible without the assistance and guidance of Heather Boyer at Island Press. I am filled with gratitude for all that she did in bringing everything together.

To my dear friends Chris Armas and Jerrod and Lakeicha Gunter: thanks for the never-ending laughs and prayers.

Lastly, to my parents, extended parents, and my family—Precious, Omari, and Khalil—I owe a tremendous debt of gratitude. I love you all.

Introduction

IN MEMPHIS, TENNESSEE, on one of five summer Fridays in 2018, hundreds of people could be seen enjoying a free jazz concert at the Benjamin L. Hooks Central Library. The music series "Five Free Fridays of Jazz" highlighted jazz musicians from across the city. In total, over five thousand people attended the series. The concerts brought together a culturally and racially diverse crowd in a city that has suffered from a long history of racial and economic segregation. The series was a programming effort of Memphis Public Libraries in partnership with the Levitt Shell (now Overton Park Shell) amphitheater, and for many attendees, it was their introduction to the library. The events provided an excellent opportunity for library staff to highlight many of the other great offerings of the library. A common refrain of visitors leaving the event was "I didn't know libraries offered *this!*"

Public libraries have long been champions for literacy and lifelong learning. They stand on the front lines of fighting misinformation

Memphis Public Libraries hosts Five Fridays of Jazz at its Benjamin L. Hooks
Central Branch. (Source: Keenon McCloy)

and disinformation by providing reliable resources and assisting
citizens in finding verifiable and accurate information.

The public library has always evolved to meet the needs of the
community. In 1905, the bookmobile was introduced as a way
to reach more children. The first one was on a wagon drawn by
horses at the Washington County Public Library in Maryland.[1]
In 1982, computers were made publicly available at the Mastic-
Moriches-Shirley Community Library in New York.[2] This would
pave the way for libraries to evolve into multimedia centers, offering not only books but also audiovisual materials, digital resources,
and Internet access. Forces such as societal changes, technological

advancements, new approaches to lifelong learning, and even a global pandemic have transformed the notions of the role of the public library and served as a catalyst for continued change. COVID-19 affected every aspect of libraries. In addition to things such as social distancing measures and outdoor and online programming, many libraries found ways to respond to the pandemic and new ways to meet the needs of the community by serving as a community partner to provide access to much-needed information, hot meals, and mobile hotspots to those in need. Libraries provided COVID test kits through drive-up windows, and in some cases—such as during my time with Memphis Public Library—staff volunteered to sew masks for those in need when there was a shortage. Libraries joined statewide vaccination efforts, and many branches served as pop-up vaccination clinics.

Libraries are becoming community anchors with a focus on bringing together diverse groups of citizens who might not otherwise have the opportunity to interact. They have become critically important agents in the civic and social health of the communities they serve. "Libraries are poised to reunite their communities, recommit to democratic practices, and reclaim their essential role as cornerstones of democracy," notes Nancy Kranich, teaching professor in the Master of Information program at the Rutgers University School of Communication and Information.[3]

At the same time, libraries are increasingly coming under attack for the services they provide. In 2022, the American Library Association (ALA) noted a record 1,269 attempts at censorship—almost double the number recorded in 2021. Most of the challenged books were by or about people of color or LGBTQ+ people.[4]

"A year, a year and a half ago, we were told that these books didn't belong in school libraries, and if people wanted to read

Memphis Public Libraries and Citizen University host CitizenFEST Memphis: A festive learning summit on how to exercise civic power. (Source: Citizen University)

them, they could go to a public library," said Deborah Caldwell-Stone, the director of the ALA's Office for Intellectual Freedom. "Now, we're seeing those same groups come to public libraries and come after the same books, essentially depriving everyone of the ability to make the choice to read them."

The role of libraries as civic institutions is critical as we find ourselves living in one of the most divisive and polarizing times in US history. Driven by hyperpolarization and partisan media, Americans are demonizing and othering their neighbors and peers, and breaking down community bonds.

The Pew Research Center reports that Republicans and Democrats view not just the opposing party but also the individual people in that party in a negative light. Growing numbers in each party now describe those in the other party as more closed-minded, dishonest, immoral, and unintelligent than other Americans.

The United States stands out among seventeen advanced economies as among the most conflicted when it comes to questions of social unity. A large majority of Americans say there are strong political and strong racial and ethnic conflicts in the United States and that most people disagree on basic facts.[5]

Compounding the levels of polarization and divisiveness, we are now grappling with a loneliness epidemic that has been deemed a public health crisis. According to a 2023 advisory from the US surgeon general, we are now seeing declines in the number of close friendships and memberships in organizations such as churches and social networks.[6] These trends have dire consequences, with the advisory from the US surgeon general noting that "over four decades of research has produced robust evidence that lacking social connection—and in particular, scoring high on measures of social isolation—is associated with a significantly increased risk for early death from all causes," and indicating that "loneliness and isolation are more widespread than many of the other major health issues of our day, including smoking (12.5 percent of US adults), diabetes (14.7 percent), and obesity (41.9 percent), and with comparable levels of risk to health and premature death." The mortality impact of social disconnection rivals that of heavy smoking (up to fifteen cigarettes a day) and surpasses the risks associated with obesity and physical inactivity.[7]

Social connection, which involves how we relate, communicate, and bond with others, isn't just a feel-good factor—it's an engine that influences individual health, community safety, resilience, and even the overall prosperity of a place. Sadly, as is being highlighted in reports and studies far and wide, many folks across America are missing out on strong social connections, and that's causing a ripple effect of issues. The detrimental effects of lost social connection extend beyond individuals, affecting performance, productivity, and engagement in schools, workplaces, and civic organizations.

What's striking is how many different population segments are being affected. Dr. Jeremy Nobel, founder of Project UnLonely, found that Medicare beneficiaries who suffer from loneliness cost the US roughly $1,600 more each year than people who are more connected to others.[8] Recent data from the Cigna Group highlights that employees who feel lonely are significantly more prone to job dissatisfaction, and fewer than half of lonely employees (47 percent) express the ability to work efficiently and perform at their peak (48 percent), in contrast to approximately two-thirds of non-lonely employees who can efficiently work (64 percent) and perform at their best (65 percent). And perhaps most interesting, that same data showed that young adults experience loneliness at a rate double that of seniors.[9]

When we lack these connections, it doesn't just impact how we feel; it touches everything from how our communities cope during disasters to the very fabric of our neighborhoods, our safety, our wealth, and even our representation in government. Social connection isn't just about making friends—it's the glue that holds communities together and creates a thriving environment for everyone, impacting everything from our health to our economic success and our ability to weather tough times.

Questions around these issues of polarization, loneliness, social connection, and civic renewal have been at the center of my professional career for over a decade, but they were heightened once I

Students from the University of Memphis Cecil C. Humphreys School of Law host an outdoor festival on the grounds of Cossitt Library. (Source: Shamichael Hallman)

entered the library profession. I joined Memphis Public Libraries in the spring of 2017 as a senior library manager, tasked with overseeing the renovation of the historic Cossitt branch. Having the opportunity to reimagine and repurpose this library in a way that resonated with the surrounding neighborhood meant countless engagement and listening sessions to hear from the community. On any given week, I would show up at the surrounding parks, farmers markets, businesses, sporting events, and festivals to talk about the renovation efforts. Time and time again, my staff and I would hear from residents who expressed a desire to

Students from a Memphis-area summer leadership program stop by Cossitt Library to tour the building and offer input on the renovation efforts. (Source: Shamichael Hallman)

connect with others but lacked opportunities to do so; their need for outlets to celebrate the cultural vitality of the community; and their mounting anxiety around being among "the other"— those from different socioeconomic backgrounds or political ideologies.

As an institution, the public library offers a resource for people of any age to find what they need to help improve their quality of life. As a place, public libraries provide a space to meet other people and be exposed to opposing viewpoints, a venue to discover new cultures and cultivate imagination. In light of the current crises that have been highlighted, the greatest attribute of the public

Participants at CitizenFEST Memphis respond to a prompt: "In what ways do you feel you have power in civic life?" (Source: Citizen University)

library may be its ability to act as a center for and facilitator of civic engagement and civil discourse, where all voices may be heard and respect is displayed for diverse opinions, thoughts, histories, and cultural heritage. This expanded role in no way minimizes the amazing work that is done by libraries every single day—and the myriad needs that they meet. This call to action recognizes the power of the public library to help address the current moment in which we find ourselves as a nation.

In their book *Better Together*, political scientist Robert Putnam and sociologist Lewis Feldstein state: "Libraries are places where people come to know themselves and their communities. . . . People may go to the library looking mainly for information, but they find each other there."[10] But what happens when they "find each other" at this particular moment in our nation's history? Have current levels of polarization created the conditions by which people have lost the capacity for tolerance, empathy, and respect of differences? Have we forgotten how to share space with others?

Ali Madanipour, professor of urban design in the School of Architecture, Planning, and Landscape at Newcastle University, says that "with globalization and international migration, smaller households and increasing variety of lifestyles, the urban populations are more diverse than ever before. As more people migrate to cities, they need essential spaces that facilitate social life, a common infrastructure of institutions and spaces that is a vital prerequisite for making collective life possible."[11] Public spaces offer a way that we might move forward in establishing social connection and civic renewal in our communities. These spaces can be used to cultivate cross-racial, cross-cultural, cross-partisan, and interdisciplinary listening, learning, empathizing, bridge-building, deliberating, and problem-solving. These are the places that allow us to get out of our bubbles and respectfully engage one another. These are the places where we can negotiate tough problems and deepen our civic health through dialogue. These are the places that create a space for us to open our minds, understand our differences, and converse with neighbors and strangers alike. These are the places that allow us to understand our commonalities, celebrate shared values, and engage in creative problem-solving.

As noted in the American Planning Association's *Planning for Equity Policy Guide*, "equitable public space sets the stage for interaction between different socioeconomic groups and can enhance tolerance and diversity cognition." But this can only happen if such spaces are designed, managed, and maintained properly. Public libraries are critical cornerstones of democracy. Due to their low barrier of entry, public libraries are among the few indoor spaces where everyone can be together.

A welcome must be extended to all—from the most affluent to the most vulnerable, and to people from across the spectrum of political ideologies. This requires internal staff training, intentional community outreach, and a continuous loop of finding authentic ways to engage with different cultural communities. High-quality physical design also plays an integral role in inviting engagement and interaction.

As affirmed by the Urban Libraries Council, an innovation and action think tank representing North America's largest public libraries, public libraries play an essential role in encouraging an active citizenry and leveraging its resources to promote human dignity, open dialogue, and respect for diverse viewpoints.

*   *   *

This book explores the critical role that public libraries play in fostering social connection, promoting civic renewal, and advancing the ideals of a healthy American democracy. I believe that libraries are one of our nation's greatest assets at this historical moment. But libraries need support to fill this expanded and often more challenging role. This is a call to action to advocate for libraries at this critical time in American democracy.

Each chapter delves into the evolving nature of these spaces, from their historical foundations to their crucial position as hubs for social connection, civic renewal, and community development. Highlighting the library's adaptability in addressing crises such as the COVID-19 pandemic and the societal challenges of loneliness, division, and disengagement, I show how libraries serve both as social and civic infrastructure, the latter being a relatively new concept. Throughout the book you will see the many ways that public libraries have met and continue to meet the distinct needs of the communities they serve. You will hear stories from library professionals and leaders of civil society organizations about the ways that libraries have become a critical civic infrastructure by taking innovative approaches to provide services that their community needs, from social connection to civic engagement.

With libraries increasingly under attack, more people need to understand their full value and potential. The book closes with steps that you can take to support your library and find ideas to implement in your library if you are working as a community volunteer.

*   *   *

My onboarding process at the Memphis Public Library (MPL) included visiting all eighteen locations in the library system to see what they were doing and to speak with library staff doing this important work. In addition to my immersive experience with MPL, I've had the great good fortune to spend nearly a decade visiting public libraries across this country—large and small, urban and rural—and speaking with hundreds of librarians exploring the many ways they serve communities. In my current role as director of civic health and economic opportunity at Urban Libraries Council, I've seen firsthand the role of public libraries in preserving, protecting, and advancing the highest hopes and ideals of democracy so that all members of our communities may fully participate in the democratic process.

Public libraries are expanding their mission to serve as an active and engaging community resource for social development and community building—a key attribute that should be better understood and celebrated.

I think that you will come away from this book thinking, *I didn't know libraries did that!*—and you will be armed with the information to advocate for libraries in a new way.

CHAPTER 1

Lonely and Divided

"I want civility."

"I want to treat others as my neighbor."

"I want to help others."

"I want to be seen."

—Mesa County, Colorado, residents served
by the library system in 2019 survey

WHEN MICHELLE BOISVENUE-FOX became the director of the Mesa County Library system in 2019, she heard the sentiments above and other similar ones from community members served by the library system. Michelle is a library administrator with more than two decades of experience in driving innovation and creativity in library settings. She had quite a bit of experience in strategic planning but had never seen anything like this. "I was completely stunned," Michelle said. "This is not something that I've seen anywhere near this . . . maybe little dribbles here and there out of research in the past, but not like this, not like this."

Through a network of eight locations, the public library system of this sprawling county serves its approximately 150,000 residents with a wide variety of resources and services. What Michelle and her team were seeing was a longing for connection and understanding in a world that has been increasingly divided, disconnected, and lonely. (See chapter 4 to learn more about how Michelle and her team responded.) As it turns out, Michelle wasn't the only leader hearing these yearnings from people to feel and be more connected.

In 2023, the office of the US Surgeon General Dr. Vivek H. Murthy issued an advisory on the healing effects of social connection and community. "When I first took office as surgeon general in 2014, I didn't view loneliness as a public health concern. But that was before I embarked on a cross-country listening tour, where I heard stories from my fellow Americans that surprised me. People began to tell me they felt isolated, invisible, and insignificant. Even when they couldn't put their finger on the word *lonely*, time and time again people of all ages and socioeconomic backgrounds, from every corner of the country, would tell me, 'I have to shoulder all of life's burdens by myself,' or 'If I disappear tomorrow, no one will even notice.' It was a lightbulb moment for me: social disconnection was far more common than I had realized." And there's data to back up these sentiments. A 2023 Gallup Poll showed that 17 percent of US adults report experiencing significant loneliness "yesterday," projecting to an estimated 44 million people.[1]

Think of a time in your life when you felt most connected. Chances are there were at least three things at play. First, there were probably a variety of relationships in your life. This could have been a combination of a spouse/partner, family, and friends. And in addition to having a variety of relationships, you probably had some frequency in your interactions with them, such as a weekly call with a parent or a monthly gathering with close friends. This, both the variety and frequency of interactions, is referred to as the *structure* of your social connections. Next, it's likely that these relationships served a number of functions in your life. Perhaps the monthly check-in with your friend provided you with a level of emotional support that no other relationship provided. Perhaps your membership at a local club or religious institution provided you access to much needed support during a time of crisis. This diversity of support refers to the *function* of your social connections. Every relationship has its shares of ups and downs, regardless of the structure and function. But as you reflect on the times in your life when you felt most connected, it's quite likely that the nature of your relationships made you feel more included than excluded and produced more satisfaction than strain. This refers to the *quality* of your social connections. All three of these, working together, produce the dynamics in which people experience robust social connection.[2]

Having greater social connection has been shown to positively influence a range of mental, physical, and other health-related outcomes. Recent studies highlight how those who are more socially connected have a longer lifespan; are at reduced risk for acute illnesses and chronic illnesses such as cardiovascular disease and stroke, including susceptibility to viruses and upper respiratory infections; and are more likely to mount an effective immune response to a vaccine. Individuals who are socially connected are more likely to engage in healthier behaviors, such as

Mesa County Libraries in Colorado host Culture Fest, which highlights the many cultures represented in the county through performances, country tables, and cultural beauty from around the world. (Source: Mesa County Libraries)

starting and sticking to an exercise routine; show better adherence to medical advice; and are more likely to have better sleep quality and quantity. Scientific evidence has tied the relationship of high-quality close relationships and feeling socially connected to decreased risk for all-cause mortality as well as a range of disease morbidities.[3]

Social connection includes a person's involvement in activities in the community or society that provides interaction with others, their sense of belonging to a group with whom they share common interests, and the resources to which we have access through our social connections.

Recent research shows that having strong social connections can influence health through psychological processes such as the sense of meaning and purpose. Adults across the globe rate their social relationships, particularly with family and close friends, as the most important source of meaning, purpose, and motivation in their lives.[4] A sense of meaning positively contributes to health because it motivates greater self-regulation in pursuing goals—including health goals. Conversely, being isolated or in poor-quality relationships can increase the likelihood that one perceives potential challenges as stressful. This stress may be heightened because the individual has less support and fewer resources to draw upon to cope with the situation.

Anyone of any age or background can experience loneliness and isolation, but not all individuals or groups experience the factors that facilitate or become barriers to social connection equally, and some groups are at higher risk than others. Some people or groups are exposed to greater barriers. It's critical to examine and highlight the disproportionate risk they face and to target interventions to address their needs, some of which include access to inclusive spaces, such as public libraries, that promote belonging and facilitate social connections.

On Social Disconnection

Social disconnection is defined as the objective or subjective deficits in social connection, including deficits in relationships and roles, their functions, and/or their quality. Social disconnection is comprised of social isolation (having few social relationships, group memberships, and infrequent social interaction), loneliness, and social negativity. Formal definitions of loneliness vary, but typically they share two common elements: an emotional component (i.e., the feeling is unwelcomed or distressing) and a social cognition component (i.e., the perception of being disconnected from other people along with a desire to be more connected). Social negativity is defined as the presence of harmful interactions or relationships rather than the absence of desired social interaction and relationships.

Robust social connection needs to have structure, function, and quality. (Think about the connections in the earlier thought exercise about a time when you felt most connected.) Without each of them, we can begin to experience feelings of disconnection and some of the negative qualities associated with them.

Social connection can be affected by factors such as mental health, socioeconomic status, and life stage. For example, physical separation from others due to circumstances such as geographical distance can contribute to feelings of loneliness. Other instances might revolve around individuals who may struggle with social skills, making it challenging for them to initiate and maintain meaningful connections. Societal factors can include norms and values, technology, and historic inequities. Community factors such as availability of outdoor space and access to transportation also must be considered. Modern lifestyles and changes in societal structures can contribute to loneliness. Factors such as limited mobility, fewer close-knit communities, and the breakdown of traditional social networks can leave individuals feeling disconnected. When all of these are viewed collectively, we begin to see the many ways that social disconnection can occur—and the negative impacts that can emerge as a result.

A 2023 report showed that over a seventeen-year period beginning in 2003, time spent alone increased while time spent on
in-person social engagement decreased. There were sharp declines
in social engagement with friends and non-household family social
engagement.[5]

Although risk may differ across indicators of social disconnection, studies find the highest prevalence for loneliness and isolation among people with poor physical or mental health, disabilities, and financial insecurity, as well as single parents, those who
live alone, and younger and older populations. Additional at-risk
groups include individuals from minority groups, LGBTQ+ individuals, and rural residents.[6]

While some social isolation, loneliness, and social negativity
are part of a normal human experience, the Global Initiative on
Loneliness and Connection (GILC) notes that "severe levels of
loneliness are estimated to affect upwards of 50 percent of adults,
and social negativity is estimated to co-occur in roughly half of
relationships."[7] The GILC is a collective of national organizations
committed to end the pressing global issues of loneliness and social
isolation. They have found that social capital—the resources to
which individuals and groups have access through their social connections—is decreasing, and fewer people are engaging in social
and religious groups. In response, the GILC has issued a set of recommendations that include the creation of awareness campaigns
that provide clear and concise information about social connection and all forms of social disconnection—social isolation, loneliness, and social negativity.[8] Additionally, the GILC has called for
increased research funding in an effort to identify and improve
interventions that prevent or reduce social isolation and loneliness
and increase social connection.

A Growing Political Divide

Recent polling data has highlighted that, across both political parties, the share of people with a highly negative view of the opposing party has more than doubled since 1994. Most of these intense partisans believe that the opposing party's policies "are so misguided that they threaten the nation's well-being."[9]

A 2017 comprehensive review of empirical scholarship in sociology, education, demography, and economics found that "growing levels of income inequality have been accompanied by increasing socioeconomic segregation across friendship networks and romantic partners, residential neighborhoods, K–12 and university education, and workplaces and the labor market."[10]

The thoughts from Michelle in Mesa County, Colorado, the surgeon general, and the GILC mirror much of what I've heard from leaders across this country—library professionals, faith leaders, urban planners, nonprofit founders, scholars, mayors of cities large and small, and residents, all voicing similar observations that something isn't quite right. These leaders are looking for bold new solutions for how we might solve the crisis of loneliness.

Sparking a Culture of Civic Renewal

In the spring of 2020, when I was with the Memphis Public Library, a diverse group of sixty-four Americans were invited to contribute our thoughts on what could activate a dynamic culture of civic renewal in America by 2030 as part of the Strengthen Our American Republic (SOAR) initiative. The group included Sikhs and Christians, journalists and scholars, professionals from nonprofits and community foundations. We were encouraged to imagine a future in which Americans from different walks of life and with political perspectives could constructively engage with one another in an effort to create a national commitment to truth, trust, reason, and civility, and work toward shared community and national ideals, principles, and values.

We were given the task of answering various questions and reflecting on a personal experience that has profoundly impacted how we see the current state of civic health in America. The answers from the personal experiences that we shared were organized into five overarching themes.

First, we discussed the ability to transcend political divisions. Despite the escalating polarization in national politics, many of us found that engaging with those on the other side of the political spectrum on a personal level often led to transcending differences. Examples were shared of communities coming together for charitable causes, illustrating how strong personal connections can outweigh political divides, especially at the local level.

Second, we delved into the disillusionment with government and institutions. In an era marked by declining trust in government and media, some of the interviewees recounted personal experiences that highlighted how institutions have contributed to disillusionment. They highlighted disparities between different socioeconomic groups in political processes and expressed disappointment not only in government but also in the media. Although technology has made vast amounts of information accessible, its influence through cable news and social media was criticized for fostering division rather than empowerment.

We also touched upon the experiences of otherness, marginalization, and stereotyping. Many of the interviewees shared instances of feeling marginalized or discriminated against due to our appearances or beliefs. Universally, we emphasized the importance of face-to-face interactions in breaking down stereotypes and fostering understanding among people of different backgrounds.

Additionally, we discussed the deterioration of discourse in society. There was a consensus among us all that civility has declined, regardless of political affiliation. Instances of encountering harsh rhetoric were highlighted, with some in the group even describing how political discussions within our families had become so divisive and heated that they could no longer be held.

Last, we explored the impact of civic engagement. Many of the interviewees had personal experiences within the realm of democratic engagement that profoundly impacted their lives. For some, this awakening began in childhood or adolescence as they witnessed a parent or mentor who had been in the trenches of political activism. Others were profoundly impacted by a shocking event or public crisis: 9/11, the outcome of an election, the aftermath of a hurricane. Still other interviewees were inspired by hearing powerful firsthand accounts of how citizen activism led to change.

While each theme resonated deeply, the topic of civic engagement stood out as particularly compelling to me, as it was the story that I shared about a 2019 conversation with a woman named Grace. As a college student, Grace, along with a few friends and classmates, made a life-altering visit to a Memphis library on a fateful day in March 1960. Accounts from librarians and patrons who were there at the time observed that the students were not loud or boisterous. In fact, these students were quite the opposite, and they were even called courteous by one patron. Shortly after the students entered the branch, White librarians advised them of the rules regarding segregation and asked them to leave. When the students remained in the library, the police were called and within a matter of minutes all of the students had been arrested. They were charged with disorderly conduct, loitering, and breach of peace. Those charges were serious enough that these students spent many hours in jail until they were able to post bond. When asked why they called the police, the librarians admitted that the reason they had the students arrested was not because they were rowdy or rude; rather it was because they were Negroes.

Almost sixty years later, I able to sit down with Grace and also with many other individuals who were a part of that story. I was able to hear their stories, see the various artifacts, and tell them directly that there would be no way that I, as a Black man, could now be managing that very same library if it had not been for the sacrifice they made. It sealed in me a desire to ensure that this library became a place where their history was remembered, where people of all walks of life were welcomed, and where conversations such as those could continue.

The summary of the interviews of the group of sixty-four (we were not given access to individual interviews) showed that the depth of division and marginalization in our country had profoundly impacted many people in the group.

A number of the interviewees noted that the 2016 election was an inflection point, leading to an increasing number of Americans who were caught in echo chambers and assumptions about what the other side thinks. One interviewee described returning to his hometown during the lead-up to the election and finding himself in heated conversations with childhood friends. This brought him face-to-face with "the profound new divide."

A consistent theme that ran through the concerns and interviewees centered on othering and belonging. Coined by john a. powell (name intentionally lowercase) at the University of California, Berkeley, the term *othering* describes a pattern of activities and structures that lead to people being isolated from and not fully accepted by the dominant society or culture, and therefore frequently disadvantaged across the full range of human differences based on group identities. The opposite of othering is *belonging*—the values and practices where no person is left out of our circle of concern. With belonging comes the power to co-create the structures that shape a community. Bridging is required to overcome othering. *Bridging* involves two or more people/ groups coming together across lines of difference (such as race and/ or power dynamics) in a way that both affirms their distinct identities and creates a new inclusive "we" identity.

The concepts of othering, belonging, and bridging have been key to my work and foundational to the work of many others. If we are to effectively tackle both the issues of social disconnection and political polarization, bridging efforts will offer a critical path forward.

In the months that followed the completion of the SOAR report, I reached out to many of the people in the group to learn more about their thoughts and community-level work on the themes of otherness, marginalization, and stereotyping, as well as stories of toxic and poisoned discourse between Americans.

Many of those whom I spoke with felt that an "us vs. them" mindset has gripped the country. And that this mindset was affecting Americans' trust in institutions and each other (at the level of family, neighborhood, etc.). Other themes that emerged touched on disinformation, trust levels, and civil unrest. As these individuals shared their personal stories, I reflected on things I had been experiencing. Being involved in conversations at the local level about disparities in how the Black middle and high school students in my community were being disciplined helped me to recognize the difficulty I was experiencing in engaging in some of these conversations, not only with those with whom I share some identity (faith, neighborhood, etc.), but also with many folks outside of my "traditional circles."

These interviewees imagined a renewed civic culture in the United States replacing echo chambers and partial truths with "creative new narratives that illuminate the rich and painful experiences of our historic and current community and national realities." They believed that these new narratives should be inclusive of the full range of life experiences and become broadly accessible through creative artistic expression. A core goal would be a focus on teaching people how to listen and talk with each other through the cultivation of cultural humility, civility, and sympathetic listening. Particular attention would need to be focused on truth-telling and healing around racial issues. They imagined a culture that elevated diverse voices in each community and elevated those who had been historically and systemically marginalized.

According to these visionary leaders, a culture of civic renewal would require passionate and skilled individuals who could facilitate conversations among diverse members of the community and train others to be proficient to do the same. These skilled facilitators, representing a diversity of age, income, faith, and more, would possess the unique ability to help people overcome differences and would have the skills needed to gather diverse folks, engaging them to listen to one another, empathize with differing views, and problem-solve. Furthermore, it was affirmed that there would need to be a place(s) in each community for these gatherings to happen. Dedicated spaces such as libraries, cafes, and churches would provide the venue for people to experience new perspectives, negotiate tough problems, and deepen civic health (see chapter 3 for more detail).

Beyond the personal question, a number of other questions were asked during the interview, such as "What is your vision to achieve civic renewal throughout America by 2030? How would you achieve this? What specific community, cultural, and institutional actions would have been realized in order to achieve your vision?" The answers that I gave then are the same answers that I give today.

Taking inspiration from great leaders, librarians, and learning networks, my vision to achieve civic renewal throughout America by 2030 is one that recognizes that America is trapped

Swing Vote Memphis was a pop-up art installation designed to highlight resources on voter registration and polling locations. (Source: Shamichael Hallman)

in a destructive loop of toxic polarization in which reflexive "us vs. them" thinking is weaponized by purveyors of disinformation, division, extremism, and hate. It is a vision that acknowledges that promoting high-quality and verifiable information and curtailing the intentional or unintentional spread of harmful and inaccurate information are as important as ever. It affirms that every person in the United States, regardless of location or demographics, should develop a deep understanding of—and appreciation for—our constitutional democracy, and that their learning should be grounded in an understanding of how to discern high-quality information, that we must engage in democratic debate and disagreement on the basis of shared truths and understanding.

Equitable access to social infrastructure for all groups, including those most at risk for social disconnection, is foundational to building a connected national and global community, and is essential to our shared success. In this diverse society, held together not by blood but by an idea, we have to be tolerant of each other and our differences.

This is a vision that emphasizes the importance of civic assets such as parks and libraries, and ensuring that they are designed for a wide range of ages, interests, and abilities, providing common ground for people to enjoy shared experiences and participate in public life. It centers on creating opportunities and spaces for inclusive social connection and establishing programs that foster positive and safe relationships among individuals of different ages, backgrounds, viewpoints, and life experiences. It is a vision that actively encourages people of all backgrounds to take advantage of public assets, through the creation of opportunities for shared experience aiding in trust-building and reinforcing a sense of membership in a broader civic community. It creates pathways for civic engagement and gives residents a major role in the planning process, encouraging them to see themselves as civic actors capable of changing their neighborhoods for the better. What I have witnessed when this happens is that early skeptics become active supporters and spokespeople for the work—and through that work, people forge new connections and engage more fully in civic life.

In particular, my vision to achieve civic renewal throughout America by 2030 situates public libraries as an integral part of a community solution. Every public library can be a place where everyone feels seen, accepted, supported, and valued. A library where all people of a given community can express their true selves, where their voices can be heard and have an impact. A library that creates the space in which everyone can better understand themselves and other people as well, address community needs, and contribute to civic priorities. The library can promote physical, mental, and emotional health of the entire community and become a space that fosters opportunity for all, builds trust, and fosters healing. A library, regardless of size or location, can cultivate a culture of connectedness rooted in core values of kindness, respect, service, and commitment to one another. It can be a space that reflects a commitment to equity, diversity, and inclusion, where people have the freedom to explore different points of view and are actively encouraged to do so.

We must unite in a collective effort to repair the social and civic bonds within our nation. This endeavor demands the collaboration of individuals, families, schools, workplaces, healthcare and public health institutions, technology firms, governments, faith groups, and communities. Together, we must combat the stigma surrounding loneliness and transform both our cultural attitudes and policy approaches toward it. This undertaking involves rethinking the frameworks, policies, and initiatives that influence communities to foster healthier relationships effectively. What follows in this book is how public libraries are leading that charge.

CHAPTER 2

Creating a Sense of Belonging

We have seen a huge uptick in incivility. The public arena has become very toxic, and I think strategically we—and this very much has to do with our media literacy program—really want to try to facilitate civil conversations between individuals . . . a safe space for a dialogue between people who may be sort of not encouraged in real life to even communicate with each other.

—Anonymous Public Services Librarian

In light of the current issues of loneliness, isolation, and polarization in our society, what are we to do? How do we create the conditions for people to connect and communities to flourish and thrive? For people to feel that they belong?

Two ideas have emerged in my work: facilitating social connections via social infrastructure and igniting civic renewal via civic infrastructure. The ideas are not new, but their importance in overcoming loneliness and polarization and how and where they are applied are taking on new life.

In *Palaces for the People*, sociologist Eric Klinenberg defines social infrastructure as "the physical places and organizations that shape the way people connect."[1] The US surgeon general's advisory builds on this definition by noting that social infrastructure refers to "the programs (such as volunteer organizations, sports groups, religious groups, and member associations), policies (like public transportation, housing, and education), and physical elements of a community (such as libraries, parks, green spaces, and playgrounds) that support the development of social connection."[2]

As part of the SOAR project discussed in the previous chapter, a definition of civic infrastructure emerged as "the indispensable community-based people, places, institutions, media, and funding necessary to build social cohesion, promote civic renewal, and advance the ideals of a healthy democracy in the twenty-first century."

It is the combination of these two types of infrastructure—social and civic—that is needed to address our crisis of loneliness and divisiveness. But first we should examine the idea of belonging—one goal of this hybrid infrastructure.

Facilitating Belonging

The first word in the glossary of the 2023 surgeon general's advisory on loneliness and isolation is *belonging*, which is defined as "a fundamental human need—the feeling of deep connection with social groups, physical places, and individual and collective experiences."[3] This definition leverages existing research on belonging and describes a new integrative framework for understanding and studying belonging, among other things.[4]

As Susie Wise explains in her book *Designing for Belonging: How to Build Inclusion and Collaboration in Your Communities*, "*Belonging* is being accepted and invited to participate; being part of something and having the opportunity to show up as yourself. More than that, it means being able to raise issues and confront harsh truths as a full member of the community. Othering, by contrast, is treating people from another group as essentially different from and generally inferior to the group you belong to."[5]

The desire to belong is a human need. Think back to the exercise in chapter 1 asking when you thought when you felt connected. What made you feel like you belonged? Perhaps it was during a family gathering where the people you are closest to were present. Or perhaps the last time you experienced that feeling of belonging was when you were with a group of friends whom you had not seen in many months, but with whom you shared many rich memories. These moments of connection come with a sense of being seen and accepted. In these types of encounters you likely feel a sense of safety. It is during these moments that you can "let your hair down" and share a laugh or shed a tear, depending on what you need at the moment. What is important was that you are in an environment where you feel that you can simply be yourself.

Now think about a time when you tried to create a sense of belonging. Perhaps you were planning a party for a group of friends. Perhaps you were planning for a weekly gathering in which you and some acquaintances get together to do some activity together such as bowling, skating, knitting, or hiking. These events flow pretty seamlessly because everyone already knows one other. But what would happen if you were tasked with trying to plan an event to bring together strangers? It would be a very different experience, one that would require some research and intentional planning to understand how to balance different wants and needs and facilitate interaction.

A sense of belonging—the feeling of deep connection with social groups, physical places, and individual and collective experiences—is a fundamental human need that predicts numerous mental, physical, social, economic, and behavioral outcomes.

In an effort to address issues and summarize existing perspectives on belonging, researchers in a 2021 edition of the *Australian Journal of Psychology* put forth a new integrative framework for understanding and studying belonging that includes four components:

- Competencies for Belonging, which deal with the necessary set of skills and abilities a person might need to connect and experience belonging. These are the sort of skills and abilities that might help a person have a richer understanding of themself and their cultural background, develop a sense of identity, and help them understand how to relate to others.
- Opportunities to Belong, which refer to the availability of groups, people, places, times, and spaces that enable belonging to occur.
- Motivations to Belong look at the fundamental need for people to feel a sense of acceptance and belonging. "In social situations, people who are motivated to belong will actively seek similarities and things in common with others."
- Perceptions of Belonging deal with a person's subjective feelings and cognitions concerning their experiences. A person may have skills related to connecting, opportunities to belong, and be motivated, and yet still report great dissatisfaction as it relates to perceptions of belonging.

What I find most fascinating about this framework is that is provides a new way of looking at belonging that not only includes subjective perceptions, but also takes into account individual competencies, environmental opportunities, and intrinsic motivations.

Adding these elements to a conversation that might neglect to account for the availability of conducive and welcoming spaces, groups, and communities where individuals can bring their "full selves" and forge connections and establish meaningful relationships can help communities to have much more nuanced conversations about fostering belonging. Looking at belonging through this lens helps to further demonstrate the importance of spaces such as public libraries as critical cornerstones of vibrant communities and a healthy democracy.

The Six Pillars of Social Infrastructure

As part of an extensive national strategy aimed at enhancing social connections within communities, six fundamental pillars and recommendations are put forward in the surgeon general's advisory. These pillars are crafted to provide guidance and assistance to individuals and organizations devoted to strengthening social unity:

1. Strengthen Social Infrastructure in Local Communities
2. Enact Pro-Connection Public Policies
3. Mobilize the Health Sector
4. Reform Digital Environments
5. Deepen our Knowledge
6. Cultivate a Culture of Connection.[6]

Several of these pillars directly impact public spaces such as libraries. Of the six pillars, I want to give special attention to the first one and the last one. The first pillar highlights the need to strengthen social infrastructure in local communities, which entails designing physical spaces to encourage social interactions, expanding community programs, and investing in local institutions that promote connection. The sixth pillar focuses on cultivating a culture of connection. Pillars 4 and 5 cover reforming digital environments and deepening our understanding of social connection. By prioritizing these interconnected pillars, communities can strive to forge stronger social ties and address the challenges of disconnection in contemporary society.

Having a robust social infrastructure, or working to enhance it, requires us to first design community spaces—the types and location of physical elements—to promote social connection. Decisions about the layout of our cities such as the availability of public transportation and the design of outdoor spaces have a direct effect on social interaction in a community. There may be a park within walking distance of homes, and getting from point A to point B is fairly easy thanks to bike lanes or pedestrian crosswalks. Perhaps, in addition to the park, there is some indoor public space, with a variety of opening and closing times throughout the week, where people can take advantage of activities that might not work well outside.

Creating or enhancing social infrastructure involves establishing and scaling community connection programs. At their best, each physical element will have complementary community connection programs such as volunteer organizations, sports groups, religious groups, and member associations. A park that you can walk or bike to may have a weekly sports recreation league where teenagers can go to compete in games and learn the importance of collaboration and sportsmanship. An indoor space that is also easily accessible may have weekly programs run by nonprofit organizations where people can learn to speak a new language, prepare

Children take part in outdoor story time at Cossitt Library in Memphis. (Source: Shamichael Hallman)

healthy meals, or enjoy a game of checkers. Let's also say that all of these programs have proven successful in that they are drawing consistent audiences that are reflective of the community, and those who attend give high marks to the quality and consistency of the events. These are the types of programs that should be scaled. In this example, perhaps scaling means that, instead of having the event only once each week, another night is added. But in some cases, these programs/events are only reaching a limited audience and people in the community realize that, due to factors such as transportation or fees that are required to participate in the activity, a number of people in the community are being left out. In these instances, establishing new community programs is needed. A robust social infrastructure only works if it works for everyone. It should be a combination of programs that ensure accessibility, affordability, and inclusivity are at the forefront.

Lastly, having a robust social infrastructure requires us to invest in local institutions that bring people together. Institutions that gather individuals for shared experiences and collective impact, such as faith-based organizations or libraries, can function as sources of positive connection and thereby bolster the community's trust in those institutions and in fellow members. Investing in community connection will be important to repairing divisions and rebuilding trust in each other and our institutions and is vital to achieving shared societal goals.

I would add two pillars: people and process. At the heart of all community programs and facilities such as libraries and parks are frontline staff who conduct the programs and provide the upkeep and maintenance needed to ensure that these spaces are welcoming. Often, these are some of the lowest-paid individuals in a given community, yet they are the indispensable linchpins who make it all work. Additional consideration should be given to ensure that these individuals are trained adequately, paid well, and celebrated as champions of their communities.

Process is equally important. For far too long, our communities—particularly those communities that are most marginalized and disadvantaged—have histories in which programs and policies have been enacted without any consideration of the hopes, dreams, and aspirations of the people who reside in them. There has been a history of things being done *to* the community rather than *with* the community. This, of course, brings about other conversations around values such as equality, equity, and inclusion. As stated in the surgeon general's advisory, "Equitable access to social infrastructure for all groups, including those most at risk for social disconnection, is foundational to building a connected national and global community, and is essential to this pillar's success."[7] Said another way, equitable access to physical elements and public spaces are key elements of a just and democratic society.

With an eye toward just cities and just environments, it is possible to see how carrying out the elements of designing the built environment, establishing and scaling community and connection programs, and investing in local institutions can lead to truly transformative social infrastructure.

The sixth and last pillar of the advisory focuses on cultivating a culture of connection:

> While formal programs and policies can be impactful, the informal practices of everyday life—the norms and culture of how we engage one another—significantly influence social connection. These shared beliefs and values drive our individual and collective behaviors that then shape programs and policies. We cannot be successful in the other pillars without this underlying culture of connection.[8]

Cultivating a culture of connection is vital to creating the changes we wish to see in our society.

Connected communities are resilient communities.

Connected communities are healthy communities.

Connected communities are safer communities.

But cultivating a culture of connection is not easy and requires a multipronged approach that not only rests on core values of kindness, respect, service, and commitment to one another, but must also take into account values such as diversity, aspiration, acceptance, and fairness. Advancing a culture of connection requires individuals and leaders to seek opportunities to do so in public and private dialogue, schools, workplaces, and in the forces that shape our society like media and entertainment, among others. As noted in the advisory, "Behaviors are both learned from and reinforced by the groups we participate in and the communities we are a part of. Thus, the more we observe others practicing these values, the more they will be reinforced in us."[9]

Civic Renewal on the Ground

Another goal of this hybrid infrastructure is civic renewal, which is all about getting everyone involved in their communities in meaningful ways. It's about recognizing that different people and neighborhoods have different needs and strengths. Right now, American democracy is being challenged. We need to empower people to make a difference and remind everyone of the importance of being good citizens. It prompts us to revisit our shared values and duties as American citizens, emphasizing both personal accountability and communal prospects for growth.

The initiative that I described in the previous chapter as part of SOAR (Strengthen Our American Republic) gathered insights and perspectives from a diverse group of respected scholars, practitioners, journalists, religious figures, business leaders, and philanthropists with expertise in civic virtue, education, and cultural and political revitalization. Supported by Stand Together, the Fetzer Institute, and the Annenberg Foundation Trust at Sunnylands, another SOAR initiative involved conducting face-to-face interviews with a range of American leaders. The goal was to explore their ideas and visions for fostering a sustainable and dynamic culture of civic renewal across the nation. Participants were prompted to envision a future where individuals from various backgrounds, regions, and

Memphians take part in Civic Hack, a collaboration of Memphis Public Libraries that encourages residents to come up with bold new solutions to existing city issues. (Source: Shamichael Hallman)

political beliefs engage constructively to reinvigorate our national commitment to truth, trust, reason, civility, and shared ideals, principles, and values at both the community and national levels.

From these interviews, SOAR developed seven themes on civic renewal that are relevant to public libraries:

1. Ground civic renewal in community. Encourage and amplify it through national institutions and leaders. Sparking a commitment to civic renewal throughout America will require collaboration among citizens, institutions, and community champions who are modeling responsible civic behavior and are actively engaging in community-based initiatives.

2. Elevate diverse voices within each community and create agency for those who have been historically marginalized. A new commitment to civic renewal will flow when all segments of the community—regardless of class, gender, race, ideology, age, sexual orientation, etc.—believe their voices are being heard, their needs and interests are being addressed, and they have agency in their communities' decisions to solve problems and create opportunities for all. This is particularly important for groups that have been "otherized" by race, religion, economic status, age, or partisan preference. When people feel that their voices are not being heard, they lack connection and agency. This is especially true for historically marginalized people whose experience is that their contribution does not make a difference in the community and the world.

3. Craft new, inclusive community narratives and spread them through creative storytelling and artistic expression. A culture of civic renewal requires creative new narratives that illuminate the rich and painful experiences of our historic and current community and national realities. Stories that are inclusive of the full range of life experiences can be told through many community institutions—schools, churches, museums, libraries, etc.—and can become broadly accessible through creative artistic expression including music, dance, performing and visual arts, and the humanities.

4. Dedicate specific community places and invest in processes for continuous dialogue, deliberation, and problem-solving. Communities need places that can facilitate opportunities for trust-building where people can practice the art of knowing and being known.

5. Support seasoned and respected bridge-builders / trainers in every community. A culture of civic renewal requires dedicated specialists with the knowledge, sensibilities, and skills to facilitate conversations among diverse members of the community and to train others to be proficient to do the same.

6. Reform and strengthen community-based institutions by equipping them with the skills and tools to promote civic renewal. A culture of civic renewal requires that existing community institutions be committed—and are equipped with capacities—to promote civic virtue, civic learning, and a sense of community and belonging as central to their core institutional missions.

7. Enhance cross-sector collaboration focused on civic life and learning among national and community-based institutions. A culture of civic renewal requires purposeful, productive, and sustainable collaboration of community and national organizations across sectors. The work of civic renewal requires a holistic, community-wide commitment by the full range of organizations that constitute community life.

Through the lens of these themes a vision of public libraries emerges in which they play a crucial role in rejuvenating civic life by nurturing a sense of belonging, active participation, and collective responsibility among community members. Public libraries already act as vital centers for fostering civic engagement at the local level. Through organizing various events, workshops, and discussions centered around civic involvement and community development, libraries foster cooperation among residents and local leaders. Many libraries collaborate with national organizations and leaders

Library visitors celebrate #RightToLibrary, a marketing campaign of the San Jose Public Library. (Source: San Jose Public Library)

to amplify the message of civic renewal and offer support for community projects. They also provide platforms for historically marginalized groups to express their perspectives and stories, thereby promoting inclusivity and empowerment within the community. Through collaborative events, resource sharing, and partnership facilitation, libraries contribute to a comprehensive approach to civic renewal in their communities. While these seven themes are the goals of civic renewal, they still need a vessel by which they can be achieved, and this is where civic infrastructure is needed.

Designing and Funding Civic Infrastructure

What are the components of this infrastructure? And how does it come together to foster a sense of civic renewal? After conducting extensive research over nearly two years, which involved observing and listening to Americans across the nation as well as engaging with leaders from various cultural institutions and experts in civic affairs, the American Academy of Arts and Sciences and SOAR identified a vibrant cultural and civic landscape thriving within communities nationwide. Their work, in which I played a small role, found some hopeful changes in this space, including coalitions that are uniting numerous initiatives nationwide to understand the practice and importance of compassionate listening in civic engagement, organizations that are facilitating numerous cross-ideological gatherings in private settings, and institutions across the nation that are promoting active citizenship, striving for an equitable and just society where individuals can fulfill their potential within the community. Yet in every instance, there was need for quite a bit more support in the way of funding and being adopted on a larger scale. As stated in the final report:

> As hopeful as these signs are, however, they lack critical mass, creative integration, and adequate human and financial capital to thrive and multiply. Ordinary citizens, community centers, leaders of local institutions, and philanthropists throughout the country are doing their best to foster social cohesion, civic renewal, and healthy democracy. However, their efforts are generally ad hoc, underappreciated, insufficiently funded, and lost in the cacophony of political rhetoric and machinations. Their work has only grown more challenging in the face of rising economic inequality and a larger reckoning with longstanding inequities and injustices at the core of American society.[10]

The report goes on to explain that our communities are currently not fully equipped to build inclusive social norms. "Without clear and demonstrable commitments to truth-telling and healing, sharing diverse stories, honoring differences, re-imagining shared destinies, and listening, empathizing, and problem-solving with people of differing perspectives, classes, and races, Americans cannot rebuild the trust necessary for meaningful and enduring social cohesion and civic renewal."

The report found that the need ("the great challenge of our time") is to (1) document these constructive community resources, (2) enhance existing productive capacities and create many more, and (3) assure that the human and financial capital necessary to sustainably promote social cohesion, civic renewal, and healthy democracy are available as quickly as possible in as many communities as possible."

We found the following four elements to be key to civic infrastructure:

1. Community Bridge-Building Capabilities. A community devoted to greater social cohesion and civic renewal requires the identification, training, and nurturing of increasing numbers of talented people with the knowledge, sensibilities, and skills to facilitate conversations with diverse members of the community. These civic leaders and bridge-builders ("facilitative leaders") must themselves represent the rich diversity of the community, be lifelong learners, and be committed to training others.

2. Dedicated Community Spaces. A community-wide commitment to greater social cohesion and civic renewal requires dedicated physical spaces—indoors and out—that are well-equipped, convenient, and accessible venues for all sizes of participant groups. These venues might include libraries, museums, schools, parks, houses of worship, sports and

cultural venues, meeting rooms in community buildings, and cafes, among others. Venues that provide safe and right-sized spaces for diverse participants enhance the facilitation of cross-cultural, cross-partisan, cross-racial, and interdisciplinary listening, learning, empathizing, trust-building, divide-bridging, and problem-solving. I'll talk more about the importance and role of dedicated community spaces in the next chapter.

3. Community Media Outlets. Increasingly, communities face the reality that responsible, community-oriented broadcast, print, and social media are indispensable for informing citizens about relevant and urgent community matters, searching for truth, and holding leaders, powerful private institutions, and government accountable.

4. Community Foundations. In order to promote social cohesion, civic renewal, and healthier democracy, citizens and institutions depend upon reliable data, objective analysis, access to diverse community knowledge and specialized expertise, and ample financial resources in order to effect change.

My involvement in the Reimagining the Civic Commons (RCC) project also helped me to better understand the role of civic infrastructure. RCC is a national initiative designed to "foster engagement, equity, environmental sustainability, and economic development in our cities. By revitalizing and connecting public places such as parks, plazas, trails, and libraries, we aim to demonstrate how strategic investments in our civic assets can connect people of all backgrounds, cultivate trust, and counter the trends of social and economic fragmentation in cities and neighborhoods."[11] RCC introduced me to the concept of socioeconomic mixing—the act of generating interactions among people with diverse economic, racial, and ethnic backgrounds. This has become a rallying cry for me ever since. Being part of these conversations helped me understand the distinct and important role that libraries could play in igniting civic renewal. I knew that libraries were playing a very important role already, but I gained a better understanding of the potential for even more work to be done (and the need for more support to carry out the work).

Libraries as Civic and Social Infrastructure

Libraries in the US are uniquely positioned to foster opportunities to make room for truth-telling and healing, create space for sharing diverse stories, and facilitate listening, empathizing, and problem-solving with people of differing perspectives, classes, and races. Along with Daphna Blatt, senior director of strategy and public impact at the New York Public Library, working over a number of months with a dedicated group of library professionals, I sought to understand how library programming, staffing and professional development, marketing and communications, community outreach, management and operations, physical design, collection development, and funding all affect a library's ability to be effective in this line of work. In collaboration with the American Academy of Arts and Sciences (AAAS), we hosted conversations with public, K–12, and university librarians across the US. Using the AAAS's 2010 report as a foundation, our conversations focused on understanding the myriad programs and initiatives that were already happening in public libraries, while also working to understand new approaches and tactics that would be needed on a local level. Public libraries in the United States function as both civic and social infrastructure. They are a hybrid of the two, unique in their ability to facilitate social connections and ignite civic renewal.

Nancy Kranich, teaching professor at the Rutgers University School of Communication and Information, and Harry C. Boyte, affiliate faculty at the Hubert H. Humphrey School of Public Affairs at the University of Minnesota, are trailblazers in thinking about the ever-evolving role of libraries, particularly as it relates to democracy and civic engagement. In the closing words of his 2006 article "Libraries as Free Spaces," Harry states: "As libraries become grounded free spaces for the information age, they will move from 'library building' to 'democracy building.'"[12]

Libraries can and should increasingly become "sites of encounters," unique spaces that can not only connect you to new sources of knowledge and information, but also provide new ways for you to interact with and understand the people in your neighborhood whom you might otherwise never meet. It was not as easy to convince people who had rigid notions of what a library could be that the library could play an even greater role in their communities. It would take a number of different approaches to bring people into that way of thinking about libraries as a critical hybrid (civic + social) infrastructure and start a process by which a community and city reimagined a public library branch to connect the community and ignite civic renewal. An important part of the conversation is promoting civic health.

Promoting Civic Health

The 2020 New Hampshire Civic Health Index defines civic health as "the ways in which residents of a community (or state) participate in activities that strengthen well-being, enhance interconnections, build trust, help each other, talk about public issues and challenges, volunteer in government and nonprofit organizations, stay informed about their communities, and participate directly in crafting solutions to various social and economic challenges."[13] While the index doesn't talk about the current state of civic health, the definition goes a long way in helping communities understand the various components of civic health, as well as various levers that can be pulled to strengthen it, such as creating opportunities for diverse connections, providing platforms to amplify local voices, implementing programs aimed at addressing community disparities or tensions, and helping people develop skills for discussing public issues constructively. Increasingly, civic bridge-building (or bridging) has been proposed as one way to achieve some of the outcomes because of its ability to promote social cohesion, foster a sense of belonging, and build resilient communities capable of addressing complex challenges in a collaborative and inclusive manner. Core elements of the bridging movement include providing education and awareness about various topics at the local and national levels where there may be strong and polarizing opinions and using various methods of dialogue and conflict resolution to help people navigate issues of complexity. Due to their low barriers to entry, robust service offerings, and the diversity of the people who frequent them each week, public libraries have incredible potential to amplify the impact of bridging movements across the United States.

Curious to explore how public libraries in the United States were strengthening civic health through bridge-building, the nonprofit organization IREX (International Research & Exchanges Board) launched the Library Bridge-Building Program in 2022. Five members of their team and I spent months speaking with people working at public libraries, library associations, and bridging organizations to better understand and possibly help to enhance the bridging capabilities of public libraries in combatting rising levels of distrust and division. We examined the success of these efforts as defined by individual library staff and/or library systems, and also identified challenges and gaps in resources needed to implement these activities and measure their impact. What we learned along the way was fascinating! Our conversations affirmed our belief that many public libraries were already engaged in this work—often driven by passionate frontline library professionals who had a keen understanding of the issues in their community and knew the potential of the library to craft innovative solutions.

For the purpose of this project, we defined *bridging* as helping people engage across differences in ways that respect individual identities, foster mutual relationships, seek a common good, and promote a commitment to civic engagement, thereby contributing to increased social capital and a stronger democracy. Public libraries provide a common ground for people who would otherwise not likely share space to enjoy shared experiences and participate in public life. As we would discover, bridging was occurring in multiple ways in public libraries, even when that specific term wasn't being used. Some libraries were already holding community conversations designed to bring people from different backgrounds together. Such was the case with the Daniel Boone Regional Library in Columbia, Missouri, through a number of initiatives such as a community-wide reading program that encourages adults to read one particular book and then participate in any number of related activities.

With their extensive collections, resources, public engagement, programs, and collaborative efforts, public libraries lay the groundwork for fostering interactions among individuals from varied backgrounds. In today's polarized landscape, public libraries play a crucial role in cultivating community spirit and encouraging organic interactions among people of different socioeconomic, racial, and political backgrounds. By engaging citizens as stewards and advocates, they empower communities to practice positive civic norms and construct traditions that support democracy and social cohesion. In response to recent social justice movements like Black Lives Matter, public libraries are reaffirming their commitment to serving as inclusive civic spaces, as is evident in their strategic plans and activities.

The most common way that public libraries are doing this is through leveraging programming, collections, and other resources to promote human dignity, open dialogue, and respect for diverse viewpoints.

A Typology of Bridging Activities in Public Libraries

These public library activities contribute to building social capital and strengthening civic infrastructure and may have either an implicit or explicit focus on bridging. It's important to note that these activities are not confined to programming. For instance, creating a book display that highlights a theme (e.g., climate change) isn't a program per se, but is an essential contribution to the learning and experience of patrons that plays a vital role for public libraries. It may be useful for public libraries, when they engage in different activities, to consider openly communicating about how those types of activities build social capital and civic infrastructure.

Public libraries strengthen social cohesion in communities and meet essential community needs in a number of ways. By offering services such as hosting food banks, supporting job searches, and aiding unhoused individuals, libraries become hubs of support and assistance for a diverse range of community members. These activities serve as more than just practical assistance; they embody a spirit of care and support for all members of the community. Through these actions, libraries model empathy and concern for those in need, reinforcing notions of mutuality and interconnectedness. In doing so, libraries contribute to the development of positive civic attitudes and behaviors among community members. However, there is an equally important—and sometimes underappreciated—aspect of these types of activities in that, by addressing foundational needs such as food security and employment opportunities, libraries empower individuals to participate more fully in civic life. When people's basic needs are met, they are better positioned to engage in other forms of community involvement, including participating in library programs, attending public meetings, volunteering, and advocating for social change. In essence, these activities not only provide immediate assistance and relief to those in need but also lay the groundwork for broader civic engagement and bridge-building efforts. By fostering a sense of belonging and mutual support, public libraries play a vital role in strengthening the social fabric of communities and promoting a culture of active citizenship.

One of the ways that public libraries facilitate civic bridge-building is through facilitating access to information, resources, and experiences. By providing free access to books, databases, and online resources, libraries empower individuals to educate themselves on a myriad of topics, from academic research to personal interests, regardless of socioeconomic status. Additionally, libraries regularly organize events and activities that bring people together, fostering a sense of community and belonging. Author talks, art exhibits, story-time sessions, and workshops on various subjects not only entertain and educate but also serve as platforms for individuals to connect with others who share similar interests or experiences. These gatherings provide opportunities for meaningful interactions, sparking conversations and relationships that transcend cultural, social, and economic boundaries. In some cases, library-organized events bring people together to do something fun (e.g., learn a new hobby, skill, etc.), whether it's exercising with friends, mastering a recipe, or learning how to take better pictures with your cell phone.

Another way by which public libraries facilitate bridge-building is through a variety of civic engagement initiatives including programs that help residents understand important historical documents such as the Constitution, meet and discuss community issues with elected representatives, or host voter-registration events, to name a few. We found that this work fits broadly into three categories.

The first category of initiatives focuses on enhancing civic knowledge. Public libraries serve as hubs for educational programs that aim to inform residents about crucial civic matters such as understanding who is running for local office, when and where local elections occur, how to comprehend ballot initiatives, and how to discern misinformation. For instance, the Civic Lab at the Skokie Public Library in Illinois provides resources and workshops that empower citizens with the knowledge necessary for active participation in civic affairs.

The second category underscores the importance of fostering positive civic attitudes. Libraries play a crucial role in promoting understanding and appreciation of diverse cultures and viewpoints, thereby nurturing a sense of community cohesion. Programs like Salt Lake County Library's "Let's Be Neighbors" initiative exemplify this by creating spaces where individuals can engage in meaningful dialogue, celebrate diversity, and cultivate empathy and mutual respect.

A civic-related display table at the DC (District of Columbia) Public Library high-lighting various resources and services. (Source: Shamichael Hallman)

The third category revolves around initiatives aimed at instilling positive civic behaviors. Public libraries actively encourage residents to take concrete actions such as registering to vote, voting, and engaging with elected officials through letter-writing or participation in local governance. Additionally, libraries may provide resources and guidance for individuals interested in running for elected office, thus empowering them to contribute directly to the democratic process. In essence, public libraries serve as dynamic community hubs that not only provide access to information but also actively promote civic engagement, understanding, and participation. By offering diverse programs that cater to different aspects of civic life, libraries play a crucial role in bridging divides, fostering inclusivity, and strengthening the fabric of society.

The last and most explicit way that we saw civic bridge-building was through activities sponsored by the libraries or by bridging organizations, which seek to create understanding across different identity groups by facilitating difficult conversations. You will see examples of these throughout the book. Public libraries serve as neutral, inclusive spaces where individuals from various identity groups can come together to engage in conversations about sensitive topics. These discussions often revolve around issues such as race, religion, politics, and social justice, which may be challenging to broach in other settings due to their potential to evoke strong emotions or disagreements. Through structured programs, workshops, or informal gatherings, public libraries provide a platform for community members to deliberate on these contentious issues. By encouraging respectful dialogue and active listening, libraries foster an environment where participants can express diverse perspectives while also seeking common ground. This process not only promotes understanding across different identity groups but also cultivates empathy and mutual respect among participants. Moreover, public libraries serve as catalysts for healing divisions within communities. By creating a safe and inclusive space, libraries offer individuals the opportunity to confront prejudices, misconceptions, and biases that may contribute to societal divisions. Through open dialogue and exposure to diverse viewpoints, community members can challenge their own assumptions and develop a more nuanced understanding of complex issues.

Bridging, at its best, fosters connections and understanding among diverse groups within a community. By bringing together individuals from various backgrounds, including different ethnicities, socioeconomic statuses, and perspectives, bridging helps build empathy, trust, and collaboration. This process can create a more inclusive and cohesive community fabric. Civic bridge-building encourages the exchange of ideas and resources, leading to a type of co-intelligence, or what my friend and social, peace, and environmental activist Tom Atlee refers to as "wise democracy"—leveraging the collective knowledge and skills of a community to address issues such as poverty, education disparities, and environmental concerns more effectively. This collaborative problem-solving approach often leads to innovative solutions that better serve the needs of all community members.

Challenges

Library staff face significant challenges to this bridging work— some of which have far-reaching implications for free speech, access to information, and personal safety (of librarians and patrons). First, there is an increasing trend of book banning, where certain groups or individuals seek to restrict access to particular books or materials that they deem objectionable. Book banning not only undermines intellectual freedom but also stifles diverse perspectives and critical thinking. And when library staff feel threatened or intimidated, they may become reluctant to promote materials that might provoke controversy, thereby limiting the prominence of differing viewpoints. During our conversations with library staff, we learned of intense library board meetings, library patrons no longer visiting certain branches because of LGBTQ+ materials, and a library director resigning due to increasing pressure about such materials.

For those libraries that explicitly leaned into the terminology of bridge-building, there were obstacles around language to navigate.

How to describe programs so that they appear truly inclusive is a challenge—librarians want to provide information, not opinions, but are sometimes uncertain as to how to do this with controversial topics. As one librarian noted, "The first year we were calling it 'fake news' and we dropped that . . . and started concentrating more on the idea of information literacy and media literacy. This fall, I completely dropped media literacy from the title because we were running into some pushback just by using the word *media*. But I think that's where I'd like to go, focusing more on digital "wellness and literacy." Other words can also trigger certain audiences. For example, *bridging, dialogue, intersectionality*, and other terms are often perceived by community members as speaking only to liberals. In October 2022, the organization Philanthropy for Active Civic Engagement (PACE) released the *Civic Language Perceptions Report*,[14] a synthesis of some of the most compelling insights through analysis of their Civic Language Perceptions data set, which determined among other things that terms such as *civil society, civic engagement*, and even *civic health* rank high for unfamiliarity, and they are also the terms that provoke the most neutrality and the fewest associations. This suggests that Americans are relatively indifferent to the terms, they may not hold meaningful connotations, and that people do not think of them as being in general usage. Four other challenges were raised in the report. (1) A perception exists that young people are negative about "democracy"; (2) a perception exists that words are "owned" by certain people or groups; (3) civic terms are favored by historically "dominant" identities; and (4) the disconnect between professional usage and public perception of civic language is real.

To overcome these barriers, recommendations were made to start with their current understanding and connect terms to the

CREATING A SENSE OF BELONGING 61

frameworks that people already know. This requires a listening posture and the ability to translate their words and experiences to civic language, and to deconstruct terms and paraphrase quickly. For instance, instead of saying *bridging*, say that you'll be putting people who don't agree with each other in the same room. Or explain that when you are using the word *democracy*, what you mean is how people govern their own lives and participate in community, not just a form of government.

The IREX team and I published our analysis, hosted a series of webinars, and partnered with a leading education platform to create a resource hub.[15] In addition to our conversations, we analyzed bridge-building initiatives, tools, models, approaches, and programs to see where there might be potential for new tools and approaches to be adopted by libraries, and we also made a number of recommendations for how to move this very important work forward.[16]

In addition to adopting language that has the potential to reach a diversity of audiences, the report recommends investing in additional supports to mitigate and reduce potential harm to librarians, including psychosocial care, security guidance, and advocacy for stronger policy in support of autonomy for public libraries to pursue their missions.

Sometimes libraries are engaged in "classic" bridging activities where people are sitting down to have a conversation about a local or national topic that is sensitive or divisive. But in so many other cases, libraries are contributing to civic bridge-building in new and innovative ways. I highlight some of these libraries and programs in the coming chapters.

CHAPTER 3

The Library as a Place for All

Public space is about democracy. The small touch points that bring people together are necessary to cultivating the calculation of democracy . . . the calculation that there is a common good, that there is moral advancement, intellectual advancement inherent to the idea of democracy and that public space has a critical role. These everyday moments of spending time together in the same space, no matter who you are, is central to the project of democracy.[1]

—Sara Zwede, landscape designer,
urbanist, public artist

CAMBRIDGE PUBLIC LIBRARY (CPL) in Massachusetts is a cultural beacon attracting students, families, and people of all ages from the Boston area and beyond. Like many libraries, it has evolved beyond a depository for books and into a dynamic "third place" for the community—offering a stunning range of services and resources geared toward the needs of the local residents. It is located in the heart of Cambridge, adjacent to Harvard Yard, and down the street from the Massachusetts Institute of Technology.

The third place is an important space outside of home (the "first place") or work (the "second place"). The third place often provides a critical social, civic, and community function. As the first and second places are blending more often with remote work, the "third" place becomes even more important. Libraries function in ways that many other third places also function, helping to create and develop social capital. But they also function as a much-needed neutral environment dedicated to guaranteeing freedom of reading and speech, as previously discussed. In libraries, people are able to be alone if they prefer, but are also able to feel the presence of others without direct interaction—helping to relieve social isolation and increase the sense of belonging in the community.

A public library's challenge, unlike other third places, is to serve the entire community, including people of different ages and abilities, at different stages in life and with a variety of needs. In my discussions with library professionals from across the United States, they have continually emphasized the importance of reaching out to marginalized groups, such as those from low-income backgrounds, immigrants, people with disabilities, LGBTQ+ individuals, elders, and others who may face social exclusion. They also highlighted the need to create an environment that embraces diversity, inclusion, and access. This often involves activities like multicultural programming, partnerships with diverse community organizations, and initiatives to foster cross-cultural understanding. Additionally, they stressed the importance of eliminating racial and social equity barriers within library programs, services, policies, and practices. This includes implementing training programs to address unconscious bias among staff and revising collection-development policies to ensure equitable representation of diverse voices. This work is designed to help more people to feel a sense of belonging. As I've searched for public libraries that exemplify these ideals, Cambridge Public Library rose to the top. As stated by their library director, Dr. Maria McCauley, when speaking of the strategic direction for the library: "We used your valuable input to clarify our mission: welcoming all, inspiring minds, and empowering community. We want to support a Cambridge where everyone has equitable opportunities to learn, people live their best lives, and democracy thrives."[2]

The Cambridge Public Library system, which includes the main library and six neighborhood branches (Boudreau, Central Square, Collins, O'Connell, O'Neill, and Valente), operates as a unified system to offer free library services and programs to residents. Each year, the library circulates over one million items, welcomes 900,000 visitors, and hosts over 2,000 free community programs.[3]

A 2009 renovation of the main branch resulted in more flexible places to study and gather—all wrapped in an inclusive design that considers the needs of library users in an increasingly diverse community. Under the leadership of Dr. McCauley, the library system has been recognized for its many community and place-based efforts, including a 2023 "Top Innovator" award for its efforts to maximize building utilization and extend library hours while minimizing energy usage to attain Net Zero Emissions.[4]

In 2023, I was able to spend some time at the Cambridge Public Library main branch with Dr. McCauley and members of her senior leadership team to learn firsthand about their efforts to be a place for everyone, regardless of ability, gender, age, race, religion, or social status.

"Everyone is welcome to the Cambridge Public Library," says Muna Kangsen, manager of communications, programs, and

Main branch of the Cambridge Public Library. (Source: Shamichael Hallman)

events. "Our values are such that we don't care who comes in . . . we just care about the behavior. If you adhere to our policies, you are welcome here to stay, as long as we're open . . . and we're willing to help you identify the resources that you want, we can help you make your résumé. We can help you search for jobs online. We can help you find the books you need. We can help you eat healthy meals, and so much more."

The library system has worked tirelessly to become an essential hub by offering resources and programs that facilitate lifelong learning. The library has made great strides in promoting digital and information literacy, ensuring that community members are equipped with the skills needed in a knowledge-based society.

"We're excited to have partnered with the city on our STEAM initiative in which we converted the old computer lab area to a tech bar area where people could check out devices." This is particularly important as CPL is located just next door to a large high school. The library offers an array of programs and services to meet the demands of students and residents alike. Take, for instance, one its newer additions, the Tech Bar. The Tech Bar is half device checkout station, half technology advice center, and offers an array of items available for checkout including tablets, mobile Wi-Fi hotspots, and digital video cameras. Items are available to borrow for a two-week loan period with two automatic renewals if no one is waiting.

Teens using the makerspace at the Cambridge Public Library in Massachusetts. (Source: Shamichael Hallman)

The space surrounding the Tech Bar is designed to enhance the comfort of portable computing, featuring relaxed coffee-bar-inspired furniture. Additionally, a new seating section called the "work bar" has been introduced along a previously underutilized hallway. Not everyone can afford electronic devices such as laptops, tablets, or e-readers. By offering these devices for checkout, libraries ensure that people from all socioeconomic backgrounds can access the necessary technology for completing assignments, conducting research, or enjoying digital resources. Electronic device checkout services ensure that everyone, regardless of their background or circumstances, can participate in the digital realm. This inclusivity is crucial for building a connected and empowered community where individuals have the tools they need to thrive.

A state-of-the-art makerspace, called The Hive, serves as a hub for STEAM (Science, Technology, Engineering, the Arts, and Mathematics) learning, creativity, and community collaboration. Its mission is to provide free, hands-on learning opportunities to the community, resources for personal projects, and the cultivation of skill-sharing and creative collaboration among library patrons of all ages. The space offers access to a variety of equipment such as sewing machines, laser cutters, and three-dimensional (3D) printers. State-of-the-art recording studios are equipped for beginners and experienced users alike. The Multimedia Studio—two separate studios that can be used to create audio and video projects—can accommodate a small group production including props or instruments, and the Extended Reality studio provides access to augmented and virtual-reality experiences. On any given week The Hive host courses such as Videography 101, 3D Printing 101: Game Piece Design, and a four-part machine-sewing workshop series led by a fiber arts artist.

A recording area in the makerspace at the Cambridge Public Library in Massachusetts. (Source: Shamichael Hallman)

This sort of novelty adds a level of freshness and creates a unique physical experience to the library, creating a destination-worthy appeal. Leaning into novelty is a bit of the secret sauce for CPL. The library, through funding from its foundation, secured a portable, induction-stove-top cooking cart that has become one of its biggest draws.

McCauley said that patrons "were already taking advantage of this space as a place to convene and hang out with their friends and eat food. So the library staff said, 'What if we bring food into that space?' That revelation led to the creation of a program through which the library brings in amazing chefs from local restaurants."

Muna Kangsen explained, "The program that we've been running right now, which we just kicked off a few months ago, is called Cambridge Cooks. And so we have the Forge Baking Company come and show patrons how to make a flatbread dough . . . and so it's like a cooking TV show, almost, where they sort of bring things that are premade, and then they show you the process, and then they pull the one magically out of the oven that's already been made and then everyone gets to try the food and takes it home with them. And they even made balls of dough that they just gave away at the end."

The cooking cart touches upon a combination of senses—taste and smell—that people don't traditionally associate with libraries. But the cart also serves a key component in fostering social connection by bringing people together over shared interests such as food, even if they come from totally different backgrounds. It has served as a way of bringing new audiences to the library.

Demand for cooking-cart-related classes has increased rapidly. And the staff is testing different ways to meet that need.

Library patrons participate in Cambridge Cooks, a program of the Cambridge Public Library, Massachusetts. (Source: Muna Kangsen)

For instance, classes geared toward helping people eat healthier while incorporating more-sustainable practices, such as decreasing food waste, are currently being developed. The library sees another opportunity for the cooking cart as a way of celebrating the cultural vitality of the community. The staff has planned a cooking-related "heritage month" program where they pair books and cooking to delve into the cuisine of whatever heritage is the focus for the event. This focus on offering joyful and inspiring experiences around cultural heritage is a key part of CPL's strategic framework.

Highlighting the various cultures of a community is one of the many ways that libraries such as CPL work to attract and engage diverse audiences. Through cultural festivals and heritage

Muna Kangsen, manager of communications at the Cambridge Public Library, highlights the library's cooking cart. (Source: Shamichael Hallman)

celebrations, libraries are able to highlight the rich diversity within their communities. These events often feature music, dance performances, traditional crafts, and culinary delights from different cultures, providing a platform for sharing and appreciating cultural traditions.

Mesa County Libraries, Colorado

"Every day we meet people who are new to the community," says Michelle Boisvenue-Fox, director of the Mesa County Library in Colorado. "And after they get their state ID [license], they come to the library to get their library card—that's how important it is to them. They ask about programs, especially things like book clubs, so they can meet new people. They want to learn about the community and they want to make connections. The library is important to them. Our story time gives parents opportunities to meet one another. . . . It's actually not unusual for me to hear stories from adults that these friendships last long after the children are grown and go away to college. That's the importance of connection."[5] In her 2020 TEDx talk, Boisvenue-Fox highlighted the many ways that the library system she leads works to meet the diverse needs of the community. In 2023, I had the opportunity to get an in-depth look at the current initiatives.

The Mesa County Library system in Grand Junction, Colorado, serves an increasingly diverse population (as mentioned in chapter 2). Under Boisvenue-Fox's leadership, the system has launched a number of innovative programs and offerings such as a public multimedia production studio and artist-in-residence space. An adult learning center offers ESL (English as a Second Language), GED prep, adult literacy, and citizenship classes. Like the Cambridge Public Library, the team at Mesa County has also found ways to leverage culture to connect the community. For example, the Mesa County Library's signature event is its annual Culture Fest. Started in 2010 by a group of immigrants and refugees who were using the library's adult learning center, the event celebrates all of the cultures in the Grand Valley. The event serves as a platform for individuals to showcase elements of their cultural identity from fourteen different countries, ranging from Norway and China to Mexico, Russia, and Ukraine. The library staff and organizers continue to hear stories from community members who attend this event and are always surprised by how many cultures are represented in the community.

Mesa County Library in Grand Junction, Colorado, hosts its annual Culture Fest. (Source: Mesa County Library)

But other needs emerged during their strategic road-mapping process in 2023. The feedback that they received from the community focused on the need for kindness and community—which was surprising to Boisvenue-Fox. In response to this, "community and belonging" became an essential pillar in the library's plan and was central to the events and activities they hosted. They built an interactive "Discovery Garden" at the branch on 5th Street and Chipeta Avenue to provide community members with education (such as compost demonstrations), food, and respite. The area features a children's garden, pollinator beds, food plots, shade structures, and a shed that uses solar panels to power irrigation. Volunteers and partner organizations maintain the gardens and host a variety of learning opportunities throughout the year. The garden harvest provides some food to local food kitchens and serves as a form of mutual aid among the volunteers and the community at large. At harvest time, residents are invited to bring a reusable bag or basket, roll up their sleeves, and pick whatever they like—being mindful to only take a fair share so that others can enjoy the produce as well. The garden is primarily volunteer-operated and grant-funded, with support from a variety of foundations, businesses, and individuals, as well as the Mesa County Libraries Foundation and Friends of the Mesa County Libraries. Soon, the library system will begin looking for a gardener-in-residence (GIR) who will be based in the Discovery Garden and will be responsible for creating even more programming.

Boisvenue-Fox said that, through their road-mapping process, they learned exactly how much the people in their community wanted a place to have conversations safely. "I had one person very vulnerably share that they didn't know how to be nice to their neighbors who had Trump signs out in their yard, and they

Mesa County Library's Discovery Garden. (Source: Mesa County Library)

did not vote for Trump. So, just really interesting viewpoints and needs."

Much like the Cambridge Public Library, the staff at the Mesa County Libraries has seen the power of using books, exhibitions, events, and programs to spark community conversations. For the staff, this is sometimes as simple as displays that highlight books about a particular topic, taking a "windows and mirrors" approach. As Boisvenue-Fox explained during our conversation: "*Mirrors* in that you have the right to see yourself in books and literature, and *windows* in that it gives people who have a desire to learn about others that are different from them an opportunity to do. . . . And reading is one of those ways that is a nice entry point into doing some work yourself, especially if you don't have close relationships with someone you can ask questions or learn from."

Another subtle way of encouraging conversation is through displaying open-question boards. Mostly posted at the entrance of the library, these conversation and question boards have become a simple way for people to share their thoughts on a particular topic or in response to a prompt such as "How do you want to be a neighbor?" "What matters to you?" and "What makes you happy?" Thoughts, which are sometimes anonymous, are shared on sticky notes that library staff monitor and also use to guide library programs and other ideas for the library.

Mesa County and a growing number of other libraries are hosting "Living Room Conversations" to facilitate conversations aimed at healing society by building relationships rooted in trust and respect. Participants can engage important and sometimes sensitive or difficult topics such as race and ethnicity, political polarization, or gender and sexuality. A six-part guide on grief explores the various stages that people go through—denial, anger, bargaining, depression, acceptance, and finding meaning. A conversation called "The Future of Work" grapples with the emergence of artificial intelligence and robots in the workplace.

Regardless of the topic, each event in the Mesa County series includes "getting to know you" questions such as: "What are your hopes and concerns for your community and/or the country?" "What would your best friend say about who you are and what inspires you?" and "What sense of purpose/mission/duty guides you in your life?" Deeper, more topic-related questions follow and include prompts such as "What assumptions have you made about others based on their politics or social media posts?" and "What assumptions could others make about you?" The living room conversation format makes it easy for anyone to host or participate in a conversation, and this relatively simple concept has been found to transform relationships between family members and communities.

For staff at the Mesa County Libraries, the opportunity to reduce othering doesn't just happen across political ideologies—it also extends across socioeconomic status. Boisvenue-Fox says, "Since coming to Mesa County, I've seen that we have a large houseless population in our area, especially in our downtown area near our central library branch. While Grand Junction is very rural in the state overall, we have very urban problems here. And so one of the things that I noted in the Central Library was language centered on *them*—othering people that are different from you."

The library is engaging in active conversations with the community around the unhoused community. Staff members have participated in poverty simulations put on by the United Way and worked to help each other to better understand the complexity of the issues and how to be supportive.

Boisvenue-Fox said, "I have an understanding with the conversations that I've had with our houseless patrons that when I get the question of 'Michelle, what's the one thing I can do to fix it?' I'm like, there's not one thing you can do to fix it, because there's like five different avenues the problem can fall under and there's not one easy fix for all of them."

There is a commitment by the entire staff at Mesa County Libraries to model what welcoming and kindness looks like—such as greeting all individuals by name, showing what it is like to create a space where all are heard and valued, which can be a particularly tough task to accomplish in any public space.

Boisvenue-Fox believes that initiatives such as these play an essential role in helping people get out of silos where they might only hear the views of certain people. And in doing so, she believes that—through programs, partnerships, physical space, and books—she can foster a sense of belonging. But these activities are also fostering two other phenomena that are needed in today's society: Norms of Reciprocity—a sense of reciprocal obligation that is not only a transactional mutual benefit but a generalized one (by treating others well, we anticipate that we will also be treated well); and Social Cohesion—the sense of solidarity within groups, marked by strong social connections and high levels of social participation, which generates trust, norms of reciprocity, and a sense of belonging.

Boisvenue-Fox believes that valuing kindness has been the cornerstone of the library's success. "So one of our library values is kindness, and that's something that's directed my entire career of public service as well as my leadership of my staff. It's highly, highly important. It makes a huge, huge difference. Having that empathy—and hand in hand with that is the smiles. Our staff really do a lot of welcoming and inclusivity just by smiling with people, just by helping them be seen. I have had people over my career more than once tell me that I was the only smile they got that day and it mattered to them. So this is hugely, hugely important."

North Liberty, Iowa

The North Liberty, Iowa, library system is one that has been hosting community conversations designed to bring people from different backgrounds into space with each other.

The North Liberty Library serves a rural population of eighteen thousand residents. Situated within the North Liberty Community Center, it shares its space with the recreation center. The Community Center is conveniently located, just a fifteen-minute drive from the University of Iowa. One of its notable initiatives, the Lighthouse in the Library (LITL) series, was launched in January 2021 by Kellee Forkenbrock, the Public Services Librarian, after securing a grant from Libraries Transforming Communities (LTC), a program of the American Library Association.[6] Since its inception, Lighthouse in the Library has hosted a number of events focusing on various conversational topics such as food and wellness inequity, cultural competency, and education during the COVID-19 pandemic. These topics are selected based on survey data collected by the City of North Liberty, ensuring that discussions address current community concerns. Engagement with community leaders has been integral to the success of LITL, with their involvement not only as speakers but also as active participants and sounding boards for event attendees. This dialogue fosters opportunities for community growth. Kellee involves fellow library staff in the planning process, holding group meetings and individual sessions to address any challenges. Post-event, the team gathers to reflect on lessons learned and to plan future events, ensuring continuous improvement.

LITL has become a cornerstone event for the library. One particularly impactful workshop, conducted in collaboration with the University of Iowa, focused on cultural competency and prompted attendees to express a greater willingness to welcome new neighbors. This event also served as a platform to introduce participants to other community programs. Kellee emphasizes the importance of learning different formats for facilitating community conversations, alternating between paneled events and workshop sessions to keep LITL engaging and diverse. She credits much of her success to supportive management and training received from the American Library Association.

Another creative program, called Pizza and Politicians, brings teens together with local politicians to learn about the importance of understanding issues that affect their communities and

North Liberty Library, in Iowa, hosts "Lighthouse in the Library." (Source: North Liberty Library)

exercising their civil rights. LITL and Pizza and Politicians are the types of events that are leading to civic renewal in the community of North Liberty. These programs are made possible thanks to the fearless library director, Jennie Garner.

"Relationships are key with our patrons and with our city leaders, coworkers, other organizations, neighboring libraries, educators, religious groups, and the business community," Garner said. "So I've been at our library in a number of roles for over twenty-five years, and I'd say the first fifteen of those years we spent a lot of time telling everyone about the services that we offered. We flipped that script when I started as director in 2014 and started asking people what they needed from us or what they need in the community, and then doing our best to provide services to meet those needs."

North Liberty Library hosts "Pizza and Politicians," aimed at connecting elected leaders with the community. (Source: North Liberty Library)

A Commitment to Diversity

In a moment where some organizations, and even some libraries, are stepping away from language, practices, and polices around inclusion and equity, Cambridge Public Library, Mesa County Libraries, and North Liberty Libraries are leaning in.

Mesa County Libraries are early in the process of planning a Year of Focus, which is set to occur in 2024 and will be centered on the topic of racism. Similar to the "one book" community-reads program that other libraries also engage in, the Year of Focus will include reading materials, activities, and events designed to thoroughly explore racism. The end result for the community, they hope, will be greater understanding and appreciation among Mesa County residents for their differences, their histories, and their cultures. "We want to contribute to the ongoing dialogue about these issues in our community," continues Director Boisvenue-Fox.

Likewise, the Cambridge Public Library has placed a strong emphasis on inclusion in their strategic planning. During discussions with members of their leadership team, it became clear that their strategic priorities center around diversity, equity, and inclusion, and this guides their programming choices. They assert that when individuals see themselves reflected in library programs, they feel a greater sense of comfort when visiting the library and a deeper connection to the community. This, in turn, fosters greater participation in civic engagement and encourages individuals to take ownership of their actions and responsibilities.

Muna Kangsen noted their focus on work to reach out to African American and other Black communities in Cambridge—families, elders, and teens. "Our archivist has done really deep work with the African American History Project, which is an organization that tries to highlight Black community members and historic

Black community members that might have been not known," Kangsen says. "Our archivist has developed a close relationship with artist Lisa Hamilton, who was working to document these lives. There is a permanent exhibition, the jukebox project, where you can hear the oral histories of people's lives. We also have these oral histories on file here to be preserved and made available to the public. Over fifty of those were recorded here in our archives. I think that is a critical example of a really deep relationship with the African American community."

This is just one of the many ways in which the library has worked to center diversity, equity, and inclusion. Over the past few years they have partnered with My Brother's Keeper (MBK), a collective of community leaders dedicated to the empowerment and success of Cambridge youths and families of color, to establish "mini–liberation libraries" across the city, in six different locations. The primary goal was not only to promote literacy but to do so in a manner that highlights the Black lived experience. Initially, they stocked each of the libraries with books authored by African Americans and strategically placed them at major intersections throughout the city. Through collaboration with their library foundation, they then secured funding to provide these books to the library free of charge. Additionally, they invited some of the highlighted artists and authors to speak at events that were held at the library. The mini-libraries have been successful, and the library's outreach team was able to introduce a new selection of authors. MBK Cambridge has now taken on the responsibility of restocking the libraries with significant input from the library.

What the libraries in this chapter demonstrate is that they are uniquely positioned to provide the opportunity for new shared connections and social interactions with groups from different socioeconomic backgrounds. By leveraging their programming, collections, community partnerships, and other resources, these libraries actively promote human dignity, open dialogue, and respect for diverse viewpoints. While books are an important component, they are just one part of the equation. A welcoming and knowledgeable staff, creative programming, and intentional community outreach work together to create spaces where entering the library itself is an act of participating in democracy. Here, people can read and learn freely, but also engage in shared experiences with others from all over their community.

CHAPTER 4

Partnering, Volunteering, and Collaborating

I've never met a library that had enough staff, and I've never met a library that had enough funding—that is one of the ways that volunteers can help us in libraries. We can utilize them as a resource to add, or expand library services to help relieve some of the burden of staff, to help install embedded services within our community, to expand our library community. Volunteers are a resource, and libraries need to be using all of our resources.

—Maggie Rose, PR & Marketing
Associate at the Barberton Public
Library, Ohio, *Successfully
Managing Volunteers with
Maggie Rose*, Library
Leadership Podcast

AT THE HEART OF THE WORK in public libraries to support their communities are thousands of dedicated library staff members. Increasingly, residents, educators, corporations, and nonprofit organizations are stepping up and finding ways to get involved.

For a civic space to be truly inclusive, the community it serves should be invited to be a part of the programming and planning. It is my hope in reading this book you now have a desire to get involved, even if you aren't sure where to start. If you are already a part of the library system or involved in some way, I hope that this material can be helpful in getting others involved. If you are a part of an organization, business, or foundation, you will find ideas for partnering to support libraries.

Levels of Involvement

Getting involved with an organization at any level requires some amount of energy and time. But there are different tiers to library involvement that can be considered, depending on the availability of time and resources.

The first tier of library involvement is to be knowledgeable of, and a patron of, your local library. Be a consumer! One of the best ways that an individual can be a champion of their local library is to sign up for a library card and get to know about all that the library has to offer. Many new patrons are surprised by what they discover. Most people are familiar with the library as a repository of books (now most often including e-books and audiobooks). But library cards will often allow access to much more, including genealogy databases, learning-management systems (which will help to teach a new skill or hobby), and "culture and adventure passes" (which provide free access to local zoos, museums, and botanic gardens). A "library of things" is becoming more common, in which your library card gets you access to everything from specialized technology (hardware and software) to physical space, such as meeting rooms, makerspaces, and coworking spaces. By using the library's resources regularly, patrons not only benefit personally but also demonstrate the importance of the library to the community. Hopefully, new patrons will not be shy about taking advantage of services such as computer access, research assistance, and educational resources. Many libraries now offer specialized, one-to-one support for budding entrepreneurs and can offer basic guidance on business plan creation, feasibility studies, and marketing research.

Two of the most popular programs in libraries of all sizes are toddler story times and book clubs. Toddler story times at public libraries provide a valuable opportunity for young children to develop early literacy skills, foster a love of reading, and engage in meaningful social interactions in a supportive and nurturing environment. Story time sessions provide caregivers with the opportunity to connect with other parents and caregivers in their community. This can lead to the formation of support networks, the sharing of parenting tips and advice, and the opportunity to build friendships with others who are going through similar experiences.

Book clubs and discussion groups provide opportunities for community members to connect over shared interests and engage in meaningful conversations. Libraries often host book clubs on various genres or themes, as well as discussion groups on topics such as current events, history, or literature. Participating in these groups can foster a sense of community and intellectual engagement. One of my personal favorite book clubs, and the one that I most enjoyed hosting in Memphis, is the "any book" club, in which members have the freedom to read any book they choose, rather than all reading the same book together. Members would then describe the book they chose to read, sharing thoughts, insights, and recommendations with the others. This format allows for greater diversity in reading choices and can accommodate a wider range of interests. It also fosters lively discussions as members bring their unique perspectives to the table based on their diverse reading selections. These events offer another opportunity to introduce people to different perspectives and ideas.

Patrons should be encouraged to collaborate with library staff. Librarians are an amazing bunch of folks, and patrons generally have a much more pleasurable experience and greater impact by doing things in collaboration with them.

Volunteering and Event Hosting

The second tier of library involvement requires a bit more time and effort. Volunteering at the library can involve a variety of tasks, depending on the needs of the library. The opportunities to get involved at the individual or organizational level will vary, based on your availability as well as the hours and capacity of each library. However, there's a strong likelihood that more-frequent opportunities will exist at the individual level. This might include shelving books, organizing materials, helping patrons navigate resources, providing tech support for patrons, or helping to host special events, such as a fundraising gala, which might only happen once or twice a year. As an example, when I looked into opportunities at my local DC Public Library system, I found four opportunities:

- Welcome Ambassadors assist members of the public in learning, understanding, and enjoying the modernized Martin Luther King Jr. Memorial Library, its artwork, history, and extensive services and collections.

- Volunteer Computer Instructors are responsible for teaching classes on how to use Microsoft Office computer software and teaching computer-based classes to the library's adult customers in support of the Adult Learning Department's workforce digital literacy training program.
- Special Events Volunteers support library events such as author talks, concerts, open houses, youth programs, and more. This is a great opportunity for outgoing library enthusiasts who have limited time in their schedules.
- Digital Archives Interns add content to the online repository, which houses photos, maps, oral histories, local newspapers, and more, documenting the history of Washington, DC.

There are often Group Service Projects, a great opportunity for organizations that wish to volunteer as a group and support large-scale projects such as shifting books, cleaning shelves, ushering at library events (author talks, open houses, and youth programs), and assembling materials.

Interested volunteers should be invited to contact the library's volunteer coordinator or administration to inquire about available opportunities. They can provide information on the application process, any necessary training, and scheduling options.

Nearly every library, regardless of size or location, will have some focus on literacy programs for children, teens, and adults, including tutoring, reading programs, and literacy workshops. These can sometimes take place as after-school activities, and quite often take place during the summer months. Supporting literacy initiatives at the library can make a meaningful difference in the lives of community members. People in the community who have skills in reading or language should be encouraged to volunteer to help with these programs. They can serve as a tutor, lead storytelling sessions, or assist with literacy events.

Another way for people in the community to volunteer time and skills is to host an event of their own or to assist a librarian or another patron with an event. Do you have a skill or hobby that can easily be explained to others? Perhaps a patron is a plumber, software developer, physician, or car mechanic and knows five to ten things that everyone in the community should know about their field. Perhaps they have lived in the community for many years and have seen how it's changed—for the better or worse. Why not share those insights? In all likelihood, your local library would be thrilled to work with someone who could design a thirty- to sixty-minute session in which they share facts and tips with the community. Or maybe you're passionate about seeing change happen in your community. Such is the case for Erika Olson, a lifelong resident of the Pacific Northwest, who was born at the Seattle hospital where her grandmother worked as a nurse. She attended Western Washington University, ninety miles north, where she graduated with a journalism degree. As a self-employed writer and project manager, Erika supports startups, small businesses, and nonprofits with marketing and fundraising.

Since March 2023, Erika has been hosting civic-related gatherings at her local library, the Bothell branch of the King County Library System. These gatherings invite community members to connect: neighbors, strangers, and friends come together for a friendly, welcoming hour to feel more connected to their community and work toward making it better for everyone. Typically, this includes a group of twenty to thirty people who spend time singing together, enjoying coffee and snacks, listening to poetry and readings foundational to the nation's history, and discussing their frustrations, dreams for the future, obstacles, and possible solutions. For example, during a *Mr. Rogers*–themed gathering, they explored the concept of "neighbor" as a verb. During the city's first-ever Welcoming Week, they celebrated the rich diversity of their community, noting that kids in their school district speak more than ninety different languages.

"People talk about 'finding community,'" Erika said during a conversation we had in June 2024, "but I think we all know at some level that we don't just find community—we create it together. It takes root where we're willing to make it and remake it, over and over again. I can't think of a better setting for that work to happen than our local libraries." Her 2023 post-event surveys support this, with 100 percent of guests expressing interest in attending again, feeling a sense of connection to others, the library, and the community, and stating that the events met or exceeded their expectations.

"Libraries have always been my go-to 'home away from home' in the community," Erika shared. "My mom was an avid reader and took me and my brothers to the library all the time. As soon as I was old enough, I rode my bike to the library on my own. Of course, I used libraries all the time as a student. Now, as a self-employed professional, I often use library space for client meetings. Research librarians have helped me track down data for proposals and projects. I can't say enough about how much I value and appreciate our libraries and librarians."

Volunteers who are not quite ready for something on this level can consider assisting another community member or librarian with a program or event. For instance, maybe the library hosts a monthly class on finances, which a community member is knowledgeable and passionate about. Many librarians would love thought partnership in planning such an event. Simple things such as helping set up a room before an event starts, greeting people as they arrive, and assisting with cleanup after the event are wonderful ways to not only help the library but also meet new people who have shared interests.

Donating, Advocacy, and Leadership

The third tier is donating resources or advocating for the library in some capacity. Libraries often rely on donations to supplement their collections and support programming efforts. Depending on your library, there's a chance that they will accept gently used books, DVDs, CDs, and other materials. Some libraries also accept monetary donations or contributions toward specific initiatives. An individual or organization interested in donating should first check with the library about their donation policies and any specific needs they may have. For individuals interested in making a small financial investment, joining a Friends of the Library group is a great next step. Such groups are typically volunteer organizations that support the library by raising funds to enhance and supplement library programming, equipment, and services fundraising, increasing the public's awareness of library resources, and doing volunteer work. Activities might include organizing annual book sales, fundraising events, or advocacy campaigns. Joining Friends of the Library can also provide opportunities to meet other library enthusiasts, participate in meaningful projects, and contribute to the library's success. Becoming a friend of the library often costs a small amount of money for a yearly membership but comes with a host of benefits, such as a subscription to a members-only newsletter, savings during annual book sales or at the bookstore (should the library system have one), and invitations to members-only events.

A pop-up library of the Memphis Public Library System. (Source: Shamichael Hallman)

As budgets are cut, many libraries are facing financial challenges. Advocacy efforts from community members can help raise awareness and support for the library. Simple things such as writing letters or emails to elected leaders and attending city council or other local government meetings are great ways to express support for the library. As often as possible, community members can share positive stories and experiences about the library with friends, family, and community members to demonstrate its value. During my time as a library manager, I would occasionally ask frequent users of the library to host a small gathering of friends and neighbors at their home so that I could share some insights into what was happening at the library and ways they could get involved. I was incredibly grateful for these "ambassadors," as I called them, since they did the heavy lifting of preparing the home and inviting guests. It was also a great way for me to get in front of an audience that might not have been familiar with the services and resources offered by the library. In some cases, it led to new users signing up for a library card. In other cases, it led to pledges of financial support.

One of the highest levels of commitment comes in the form of joining an advisory committee or library board. While these positions are in some cases falling victim to the culture wars, having people in these roles who understand the true impact and importance of the library as an inclusive public space is critical. For community members interested in serving at this level, I encourage them to attend any public-facing meetings and take time to meet existing board or advisory members.

Partnering with Organizations

A number of organizations are also dedicated to the work of combating current levels of polarization and division, and they provide training and resources that can play a pivotal role in promoting and fostering social cohesion. I have worked with each of the programs described below and can attest that they are always looking for ways to weave their programs and resources into libraries.

Essential Partners

The not-for-profit Essential Partners (EP) has been woven into the fabric of communities since its inception in 1989. EP believes in the power of trust, recognizing differences not as barriers, but as sources of strength waiting to be tapped. Through a variety of training, resources, and continuous feedback loops, they collaborate with civic groups, schools, faith communities, and others to build a culture of connection, mutual understanding, and trust across differences of values, beliefs, and identities.

EP hosts open workshops virtually each month to train people on how to facilitate dialogue in their local community. The two main workshops are basic facilitation and an introduction to dialogue across difference. In the two-day Basic Facilitation Workshop, participants learn tools to hold space for tough conversations in daily life, in the community, and in the workplace, using the organization's Reflective Structured Dialogue method. The daylong Introduction to Dialogue Across Difference workshop is designed to help participants envision what a better conversation about tough issues might look like in their community or organization. It can begin to break destructive communication habits in the community, campus, congregation, or organization. While the registration cost for Essential Partners is among the highest, the organization provides a limited number of partial or full scholarships for each workshop it hosts, based on financial need and potential for impact on a community level.

I was drawn to the work of EP after meeting John Sarrouf, co–executive director, in 2020. At the heart of their work is Reflective Structured Dialogue (RSD)—a flexible, research-based, scalable framework for systemic change. RSD equips people to interrupt dysfunctional dynamics and build relationships across differences in order to address challenges where they live, work, worship, and learn.

The combination of informal and formal influences has the power to change the culture of the group, school, or institution as well as the larger community and the broader society. A few years ago I had the privilege of being trained in a newly developed program called PhotoVoice—a multimedia version of EP's Reflective Structured Dialogue methodology, incorporating elements of a visual/narrative storytelling and bridge-building. The training wove together dialogue skills with a process for generating reflection and conversation through visual prompts. For example, participants in one session introduced themselves with photos that they took in an effort to help others understand something about themselves and their communities, such as pictures of a community garden, park, or concert venue. Other participants added comments and questions, which then served as springboards for dialogue. The process often allowed participants to explore the difficult or persistent challenges they face in their communities. PhotoVoice is helpful in drawing in a diversity of people to the library. It has been estimated that the average cell phone user has two thousand photos on their phone! Creating a safe space in which people can share photos while also talking about community and societal issues that they are passionate about is a no-brainer.

Katie Hyten, co–executive director of EP, has served in roles of fieldwork, training, facilitation, and coaching, both internally and externally. EP's work has thrived in the heart of communities, where people have grappled with their most pressing challenges, and Katie recalled seeing this unfold in many ways:

> Also what we look at is actually in every space there are going to be people where differences interact in some way. Those differences may be political, red, blue, they may not be, they may intersect, they may be much more complex than that. And I think for us, we really want to bring back in that complexity that allows people to be seen by the varied experiences and identities and beliefs that make them who they are, and then hold

them with a blend of conviction and humility to be able to say, yes, this is what I believe and here's why this is important to me and why this matters to me, but also I'm going to hold it with humility and know that I don't know everything because no one knows everything, and be open to building those relationships [in order to develop] that long-term focus—that deep, deep focus in helping people shift how they engage across differences and creating opportunities for people to do that in their everyday lives.

Hyten recounted EP's early foray into the fraught terrain of abortion discourse, where traditional approaches had faltered. Rather than aiming for agreement, they championed dialogue as a means of building trust and understanding. It was a lesson that reverberated through the years—a reminder that even in the absence of consensus, relationships could endure and communities could flourish. At the core of it all is a commitment to intentional dialogue, a recognition that every voice matters, and every perspective holds value.

A library is a place where people come to work, access the Internet, and stay warm. It's where people come for events, programming, and learning opportunities. And it's a place of gathering for people where people are being held and where people are holding space all the time. And then I think it's a place where people connect with other parts of both their communities. We see a lot of work happening that goes beyond the boundaries and the borders of the schools. They're connecting with congregations that are hosting bible studies, that are hosting community events, that are working alongside after-school programming and boys and girls clubs and YMCAs. . . . If you were to map any city or town in the United States, the tendrils that come to and from the library are just hard to imagine. And I think that's what makes libraries so well suited for this work, because people are already engaging with the library in so many different ways, and it's such an important part of our community life. It is really, truly a cornerstone of community life in the deepest sense.

Human Library

"I started getting into this work around 2016 . . . wanting to find ways to bring people together across perceived differences," says Ben Caron. "I felt like I was witnessing, especially in the United States, an increase in divisiveness and a lack of compassion and empathy for folks that we perceive to be different from us." One of the ways that Ben has been engaged in this effort is through his work with the Human Library; an international nonprofit organization that was started in Copenhagen, Denmark, a little over twenty years ago with a simple but radical mission: to create safe space for courageous conversations. Ben currently works in a number of roles with Human Library including facilitating a number of trainings for the organization, organizing and leading on all events in Los Angeles, coordinating private events in workplaces across the United States, and producing a series of free online events for the public.

With a tagline of #unjudgesomeone, the organization has worked to create a process that equips anyone who wants to bring people together to have courageous conversations. And they accomplish this partly by centering people who have experiences of prejudice, stereotype, marginalization, or hardship. The Human Library team works diligently to identify people with these specific experiences because they find that those are the things we don't talk about openly in society. In essence, they are trying to create a space where those conversations are centered.

Events are held in various settings, from libraries to workplaces, where trained facilitators, or "librarians," guide participants, known as "readers," through dialogue with volunteer storytellers, termed "human books." The conversations, aptly termed "readings," unfold organically. There are no scripts, no monologues—only dialogue. Readers are encouraged to ask, to probe, to explore the depths of their curiosity. For thirty minutes, they engage in a dance of words, guided by mutual respect and a shared commitment to growth. Yet the journey begins long before the first word is spoken. In collective orientations or one-on-one conversations, the librarians foster trust and agreement among participants. They ensure that everyone feels heard, understood, and valued—a testament to the dedication to maintaining safety and respect throughout the experience.

Ben states,

It's a safe space for you to ask things that you maybe were scared to ask in other settings. It's a safe space for you to take risks. It's a safe space for you to get something wrong. We find in the organization that oftentimes what keeps people from the conversation in the first place is they're so scared of offending somebody. They're so scared of getting something wrong. They're so scared of revealing that they're a beginner, that they'll stay away from the conversation altogether to sort of protect themselves from those experiences. And so we create a space where you are encouraged to take risks, where you're encouraged to be vulnerable, you're encouraged to be courageous, and you're encouraged to ask the questions that maybe would be inappropriate even to ask in other settings.

Expressing genuine fondness for librarians and administrators, Ben underscored their shared ethos of service and dedication to public welfare. The synergy between Human Library teams and library staff, he emphasized, was characterized by mutual understanding and collaboration toward a common goal. For Ben, the Santa Monica Public Library stood out as a beacon of excellence in Los Angeles, while the Kenosha Public Library in Wisconsin and the Mesa County Public Libraries in Colorado exemplified remarkable dedication and innovation in community service—each partnership a testament to the enduring impact of collaboration in shaping a more inclusive and compassionate society.

One of the things that I have most admired about the Human Library is that it both provides an opportunity for people to meet others from totally different backgrounds and provides a space for people to see themselves. I've personally seen how amazing these events are, and the public library is an ideal location to host them.

Civic Saturday Fellowship

Hosted by Citizen University, this free six-month program equips engaged and inspiring Americans to create purposeful rituals and root them in community-centered ways. Participants learn, practice, and host a series of Civic Saturday gatherings in their community. From Philadelphia to San Francisco to rural parts of Tennessee, Civic Saturday Fellows are bringing people together to dedicate themselves to the practice of powerful, responsible citizenship. The team at Citizen University hosts this training multiple times a year. Having gone through the fellowship myself in 2019, I can attest that this is a wonderful way of bringing your community together.

The Civic Saturday events often include readings, music, and guided discussion. The readings are often of historical texts crucial to the formation and development of our country by people such as Susan B. Anthony, Frederick Douglass, and Alexis De Tocqueville, as well as urban advocates such as Jane Jacobs. There is poetry, music, shared reflections, and facilitated discussion on topics related to democracy, citizenship, and community values. When I first started hosting these events, they were confined to meeting rooms in the back of the library. But on one occasion a library branch manager asked if I could host in the main "public area" of the library. She knew that this could be a huge disruption to people who were studying or using the public computers, but she thought it was worth the gamble. A few days before the event, she put up signs all throughout the library informing the library patrons that things would be a bit noisy for a few hours on the upcoming Saturday. To our surprise, not only did people not complain about the music and poetry readings, but they stopped what they were doing and joined in! From that point forward, I always sought to host the gatherings in the most public part of the library. It has proven to be a wonderful way of engaging a diverse group of people who have all come to the library for different reasons. And that is what I believe is the real reason why hosting these events in the library works so well. Civic Saturday gatherings present a tremendous opportunity to facilitate transformative conversations and build relationships with people who might not otherwise interact. Since going through the program, I have met countless individuals who did the same and are now hosting Civic Saturday gatherings a few times a year at their neighborhood library branch.

Library patrons participate in a Civic Saturday gathering at Memphis Public Library. (Source: Shamichael Hallman)

Living Room Conversations

Living Room Conversations aim to foster connection within communities and bridge divides in order to increase understanding, respect, and empathy. Libraries are a perfect place to host such conversations. The program has more than 150 free conversation starter guides, which provide detailed steps on how to have conversations about a number of topics such as Civic Renewal, The American Dream, and Anxiety and Elections.[1] There are also a number of conversation starter guides on what might be considered less "charged" topics—The Search for Purpose, Loss and Grief, and Gratitude. The conversations are centered around "conversation agreements," presented at the beginning of each gathering, in which participants are urged to approach with genuine curiosity and active listening. Participants also pledge to withhold judgment, fostering an environment where everyone feels esteemed and honored. Lastly, in an intentional effort to be mindful of others, participants are asked to ensure that there is equal time for everyone to speak and actively look for common ground or shared values that may emerge during the conversation.

Hosting a conversation is as simple as selecting a topic, gathering four to six people to talk about it, following the conversation guide and agreements, and answering questions based on your experience with the topic, not based on your opinion.

Programs such as these present a tremendous opportunity to positively shape communities when hosted by or in collaboration with public libraries. These initiatives help to create environments where people feel fully listened to and respected. Investing in social connections, within and between groups, strengthens community bonds and promotes well-being. Benefits are realized from fostering connections with diverse individuals and groups and reflecting on ways to nurture social capital to enhance abundance and collective thriving.

The closing remarks of the US surgeon general's *Advisory on the Healing Effects of Social Connection and Community* emphasize that addressing the loneliness epidemic requires collective effort, involving everyone from individuals to larger communities.[2] Each person has a role to play, beginning with recognizing the impact of social connection and the risks of disconnection and polarization. One effective way to achieve this understanding is through civic engagement, such as volunteering at your local library. Volunteering at the library allows individuals to actively participate in and contribute to their community's well-being. It promotes literacy and lifelong learning while fostering opportunities to meet new people, make friends, and build meaningful relationships. Overall, volunteering at the local library is a reward-ing way to give back, support education, and positively influence others' lives.

Encouraging active listening and seeking common ground are essential for building consensus and unity. Getting involved with your local library offers various avenues to playing an important role in creating a more inclusive and equitable community. How-ever, it's crucial not to remain passive but to actively engage in initiatives that benefit the community.

The Citizen as Artist

Eric Liu, who wrote the foreword to this book, is founder of Citizen University and author of some powerful books on what it means to be a citizen. Eric has been a close friend, a mentor, and one of the most inspiring people in my life. In his 2019 book *Become America: Civic Sermons on Love, Responsibility, and Democracy*, he has a chapter on the citizen as artist. He describes this intersection between citizen and artist:

> Citizenship is art. Many Americans, under the category "citi-zen," have the mental model of the janitor or the judge or the Scout or the Samaritan. But the model that fits best is the artist. I want you to leave today and tell the people you know that they are artists composing a community, devising a country, work-shopping a *We* using nothing but a random pile of little Me's and the flimsy wire frame of the Constitution.[3]

Eric goes on to state that

> to be a citizen is to put out a call and listen for who shouts it back. To be a citizen is to invent new hybrid forms out of what we find lying around. To be a citizen is to turn fragments of

thought into poetry with the compact sharpness of arrowheads. To be a citizen is to use the bare frames of structure to spur improvisations. To be a citizen is to make the rituals that make a nation. To be a citizen is to convert absolute awfulness into hope and hope into power.[4]

*   *   *

I am encouraged by the people I have seen and befriended across this country who are finding their own way of *showing up* and creating the world they wish to see. If the citizen is indeed an artist, then may the public library be the art supplies by which a beautiful picture can be painted.

CHAPTER 5

Lessons from Memphis

It's changed everything for me. Sometimes I have to stop myself and say, "Wait a minute, this is all happening at the *library*? And it's all free?"
—Tim Felix as quoted in *Smithsonian*,
"How Memphis Created the
Nation's Most Innovative
Public Library," 2021

IN 2021 MEMPHIS PUBLIC LIBRARIES (MPL) became the first institution to win the national medal by the Institute of Museum and Library Services (IMLS), making them the first two-time winner (2007, 2021). Selected from thirty national finalists, the 2021 National Medal for Museum and Library Service winners represented institutions that provide dynamic programming and services that exceed expected levels of service. This signature IMLS program is one of the highest honors that an American library or a museum can receive.

MPL's eighteen branches serve over two million people in one of the most economically challenged cities in the United States. As noted by then director Crosby Kemper during the award service, MPL offers countless programs that "focus on the underserved and bridging the digital divide. Through their community outreach, these institutions bring about change that touches the lives of individuals and helps communities thrive."[1] In addition to the numerous programs and outreach services that were recognized, the renovation efforts of its historic downtown library branch were also honored.

In 2019, the Memphis Public Library undertook a full renovation of the historic Cossitt Library branch, located in downtown Memphis. This branch, established in 1893, was the first in the Memphis system, and the first Southern library to be desegregated.[2] The library leadership worked with the community to advance the role of the library as a community anchor and a catalyst for civic engagement. We worked to develop programming designed to bring together diverse groups of citizens who otherwise might not have the opportunity to interact or learn from each other. The downtown area was home to both many affluent residents and a sizeable unhoused population. The Memphis Public Library was able to experiment and thrive, thanks in part to community participation, strong leadership, an amazing group of architects, designers, and builders, as well as strategic investments and exposure to a transformative set of people, places, and ideas across the United States. I was brought in to help lead the renovation in 2017.

The renovation efforts were part of a bold new national initiative, Reimagining the Civic Commons (RCC), that was investigating the potential of public spaces to anchor, uplift, and revitalize communities. Since 2015, Reimaging the Civic Commons has brought together practitioners, advocates, policymakers, and residents to advance new ways of designing, managing, and measuring public spaces. Housed at U3 Advisors, the Learning Network provides this growing community of practice with access to research and impact assessment, elevation through storytelling, and opportunities to learn from other cities pursuing this important work.[3]

Weaving in elements from the RCC outcomes, such as civic engagement and socioeconomic mixing, the Memphis Public Library, along with Groundswell Design Group, distilled a new concept for the renovated branch into three simple three words: *Learn. Connect. Share.* From those three words, a simple yet powerful concept statement emerged:

> In the heart of Memphis, the Cossitt Library is designed to adapt to the ever-changing needs of the community. The spaces transform to accommodate diverse neighborhood endeavors: creating an unrestricted landscape for myriad social engagements, workshops, presentations, and artful installations. Local artists, professionals, and instructors gather to exchange expertise. In this way, the community shapes and gains ownership of Cossitt Library, guiding its dialogue and rendering it uniquely Memphis.[4]

Undergirding the work of the RCC learning network are four outcomes that guide new approaches to public space:

- Civic Engagement—Building a sense of community that brings people of all backgrounds back into public life as stewards and advocates, shaping their city's future.
- Socioeconomic Mixing—Creating places where everyone belongs, and that generate opportunities for shared experience among people of all incomes and backgrounds.

- Environmental Sustainability—Increasing access to nature and creating environmentally friendly places, easily reached by walking, biking or transit.
- Value Creation—Encouraging additional investments in neighborhoods so that they are better places to thrive.

A number of metrics and signals were created to help measure the goal of socioeconomic mixing. For instance, a "mixing on site" metric takes into account the probability that any two individuals selected at random will be from the same income group (with a goal of being as diverse as possible) as well as the percentage of site visitors within conversational distance of one another. Another metric, "bridging social capital," looks at the percentage of visitors making new acquaintances, and the corresponding opportunities for meeting new people. According to Amanda Miller, learning network expansion manager for Reimagining the Civic Commons:

> Socioeconomic mixing can be as simple as sharing space with people of different backgrounds or the small casual interactions that happen when we encounter others in public. To put it simply, the more we inhabit space with and interact with others who have different lived experiences, the greater capacity we have to develop the connections that create greater access to opportunity—and build a future in which everyone benefits.[5]

Visits to other cities that were part of the RCC Learning Network, including Detroit, Chicago, and Akron, helped me understand how practitioners were working to achieve socioeconomic mixing in public spaces in their communities. There was no other representative of a public library in the RCC, but I was able to contextualize the key learnings from these cities and convert them into opportunities and ideals for the library profession. The combination of our visits to other cities as part of the civic commons learning network, as well as visits to award-winning libraries across the country, helped us create a winning formula for the renovated library.

Reimagining a Space Centered on Belonging

There were five actions that the Memphis Public Library took to create a space centered on belonging: (1) create new narratives about the role of the library; (2) feature local art and artists; (3) work to connect diverse local cultures; (4) hire a diverse staff; and (5) research and pilot a variety of programs to achieve the goal of socioeconomic mixing.

1. Create new narratives about the role(s) of the library.

A 1992 cover story in the neighborhood newspaper, the *Commercial Appeal*, reported that Cossitt Library, after nearly a century downtown, had emerged as "the library branch with the richest history, but poorest future."[6] Many of those sentiments persisted even after the building renovation was begun in 2019. In our early community engagement efforts with residents in the immediate vicinity, some mentioned that they hadn't set foot in the Cossitt Library in years, while others mentioned that they didn't even know the library existed. Shifting the narrative of this space would not only require an amazing design, but a new vision of what it could be in the community. That vision would have to change user perceptions of the space, perceptions of who belongs in the space, and perceptions of what was possible in the space.

We started this process by identifying the library's key goals from the 2020–2025 strategic plan, which centered on enhancing equitable access to educational, service, and cultural resources, championing literacy for all, and promoting economic advancement and workforce development to help break the cycle of poverty.

These were values that we used as rallying points in our community engagement sessions. In addition to the library's strategic plan, we were able to incorporate language from the RCC initiative, which highlighted key themes around topics such as creating a sense of welcome for people of all backgrounds and shifting the behavior of citizens from consumers to producers in order to steward and champion our public assets. Lastly, we had the concept statement from the design team for the library, Groundswell Design Group.

To create a new narrative, the staff and the community needed to embrace elements of aspiration and to believe that we could create something in this library that hadn't quite been seen in a library before. At least not in Memphis. We would need to allow creativity and experimentation to take us to new places.

Artist Ean Eldred of rhiza A+D converses about the creation of a sculpture to be placed on the grounds of Cossitt Library. (Source: Shamichael Hallman)

We experimented with noise—certainly the library didn't always have to be a quiet space.

We added food. Delicious, destination-worthy food prepared by a local chef.

We replaced wooden shelves with rolling bookshelves so that we could alter the physical space to accommodate many different offerings.

We offered unique equipment such as virtual reality (VR) headsets that could provide immersive experiences into new worlds. Now, not only can patrons read about foreign lands in books, they could put on a headset and see it for themselves.

We offered coworking options for those who were remote or hybrid workers.

We piloted a process by which the collection of books could change and rotate, based on times of the year.

We extended operating hours so that the community had more options to visit.

We created a place of beauty that would be accessible to all.

We hoped to generate enough excitement to get people to think about the library differently. Yet success meant that everyone might show up, so it became necessary for us to foster values rooted in belonging, respect, and inclusion. If we were to be successful, everyone—regardless of age, race, gender, sexuality, or income—would need to feel accepted and comfortable. The library would need to be firm about being a place that accepts differences and honors different voices, opinions, behaviors, and cultural expressions.

And yet we knew that providing wonderful amenities and state-of-the-art technology could lead to the community having a highly transactional view of the space and could result in a dynamic where the library was seen only as a place where you go to *get*. We wanted to push against that narrative and help the community to see that the library was a place where they could go to *give*. To achieve that, we had to embed notions of engagement and participation into our new narrative. Whether it was through joining the Friends of the Library group or signing up to host a program, we wanted people to know what would truly make the library special would be a place that was steeped in relationships.

2. *Feature local art and artists to inspire and engage the community.*

Memphis has an innovative and thriving arts culture, from dance, to music, to fashion. It was important for us to acknowledge the role of art and artists in Memphis and use the library to celebrate and support artists and highlight their works.

A community listening session hosted by Memphis Public Libraries. (Source: Shamichael Hallman)

Our first step was to create an engagement plan targeted at artists, arts organizations, and creative entrepreneurs in the city so that we could learn about their work and understand the challenges they were facing. We invited artists to the building during the renovation process so that they could see firsthand the various spaces in the building and some of the resources that would be available, and get their thoughts on what they needed. The feedback that we received led to a few minor changes in the design of the building, such as a more flexible lighting grid, but more importantly it helped us understand new ways of supporting these artists. For instance, we learned that there was a need for equipment and resources to support podcasting, which the artists were using as both a medium for their work, such as through the creation of audio dramas, and a platform to amplify their work. We were able to purchase equipment (microphones, recording software, and an integrated audio production studio) and books that could support this work and explore ways to build out and staff the audio recording space. We worked to secure the best possible equipment that we could afford and worked with an audio engineer to ensure that the recording spaces had all of the necessary acoustic buffering and sound-absorption characteristics. Individuals would be able to reserve space, browse a selection of books on the topic, and have access to professional podcasters and individuals with experience in the audio recording profession such as Ralph Calhoun, a library employee and audio engineer coordinator who had worked in studios in Memphis and Nashville.

The audio recording space was of particular interest to many of the individuals who received tours of the building. There was demand for space many months before it was available for public use.

We mirrored this process for the photography and video recording space. The space was flexible, with equipment available such as green screens, lighting kits, and 4K cinema cameras. We hired a nationally recognized photographer—someone who had previously worked with companies such as Gap—to offer a variety of classes, workshops, and product demonstrations.

These two spaces were not the only draw for creative entrepreneurs and artists. A workshop and coworking area of approximately a thousand square feet was available. Libraries have long provided space and resources for entrepreneurs and individuals to work and conduct business—in some ways libraries are the original coworking space. Functioning as both a coworking space and makerspace, this unique area of the library attracted artists in mixed media, textiles, ceramics, and leather goods. We offer a variety of equipment such as sewing and embroidery machines, sublimation printers, heat press machines, and printable vinyl sheets. To this we once again added an array of books, magazines, and online resources—all of which can be used for free with a library card—so that visitors can gain new skills along the way.

While we are still understanding the true impact of having these spaces and equipment made freely available, there are two things that we know for certain from the direct feedback from patrons of this space: (1) the availability of this equipment has leveled the playing field for artists and creative entrepreneurs in the city because they now have access to equipment that might have otherwise been out of reach due to financial constraints; and (2) having a flow of creative people who are using the library to produce, create, and share their work has created an atmosphere where many more people, of all sorts of backgrounds and from different parts of the city, are now visiting and using the library because of the energy that is present.

While we felt good about the combination of design and equipment to draw in artists and creative entrepreneurs, we knew that there was more work to do. So, starting in the summer of 2021, we embarked on a series of community conversations with local artists and arts organizations to get input about the performance space and the recording areas in order to more deeply understand how the renovated library could help to meet their needs. Led by Emily Marks, a library staffer who is also an amazing artist, we engaged over 100 artists and creatives, representing individual practices, small companies, organizations, and established institutions—ranging across disciplines from music, theater, film, dance, culinary art, and more. In addition to local artists, Emily also reached out to public library systems in New York and Las Vegas–Clark County that had already implemented very progressive policies as they relate to working with artists.

From those conversations, three key findings and four recommendations emerged. We found that:

- Our library could invite and embrace diverse cultural voices. Artists were excited about the rich history and legacy of Cossitt Library, and they embraced many of the ideas we had about the role we could play in their lives as well as in the life of the community.
- Our library could be a community and support network for those who didn't have support elsewhere. Artists recognized that they could be part of cultivating new audiences for the library and, in turn, also engage new audiences with their work. It would be a win-win scenario.
- Our library could influence the economic sustainability of artists and creatives in the city. Artists were interested in accessing library resources to help advance their entrepreneurial pursuits.

Ena Esco, Innovator-in-Residence at Cossitt Library, hosts an event for area pod-casters. (Source: Shamichael Hallman)

In light of the findings, four recommendations were made:

A. Create multiple points of access to the performance space.
While there was no charge for nonprofit groups whose meetings were open to the public, there were instances where these groups wanted to use the building for private events. Additionally, for-profit businesses expressed interest in hosting various events in the space. We learned from other library systems that it would be important to have dynamic pricing models for room and space rentals dependent on the project or the type of organization that was requesting the space. Rates needed to be reasonable while still generating revenue

that could be reinvested in the space. We also learned about using a co-op model whereby artists could access the performance space free of charge in exchange for providing programming for other branches in the library system. The beauty of this model is that not only does it provide our venue and space for artists to do their work, but it also serves as a great way of ensuring that the arts make it to each of the eighteen locations of the Memphis Library system.

B. **Establish a community-based artist advisory council.** The creation of an intergenerational task force that includes community-based artists ensured that staff would have guidance on the best ways to create policies and procedures that will really work for artists.

C. **Provide professional development for artists at the library.** The idea here was to leverage existing relationships and partnerships to assist artists with grant writing, artist statements, entrepreneurial development, and more.

D. **Use local art to engage audiences in exciting new ways.** In addition to centering the role of artists in the library, we also added two works of art in and around the library. As noted by Urban Art Commission on their website:

> UAC partnered with the City of Memphis to produce a large sculpture that attracts and engages both Memphians and visitors alike to the newly renovated Cossitt Library. Rhiza a+d's sculpture does exactly that by invoking the library's history of being a key gathering and learning space. Their design, based upon pop-up books and childhood fantasies of words brought to life, is meant to invoke feelings of discovery and imagination.[7]

Ean Eldred and Peter Nylen of rhiza A+D install a sculpture on the grounds of Cossitt Library. (Source: Shamichael Hallman)

This sculpture played a significant role in establishing a sense of welcome for the library. Not only did it serve as a visual element that captured the attention of people as they walked by the branch, but the interactive nature of the sculpture also actually resulted in people coming into the courtyard to take selfies and read the various quotes. These actions generally led to people either spending additional time in the courtyard or in some cases coming inside the building.

Once inside, visitors were treated to a second piece of art—a striking mural painted by artist Anthony Lee. This mural captures a pivotal moment in the city's history: the courageous efforts of civil rights attorneys defending students arrested in 1960 for participating in sit-ins to integrate Memphis's segregated public libraries. These sit-ins were sparked by a lawsuit filed in 1958 by Jesse Turner and H. T. Lockard. Turner, a prominent CPA and influential figure in the early civil rights movement of the city, had experienced first-hand the injustice of segregation when he attempted to enter the Cossitt Library and was turned away because of his race. Just as the exterior sculpture plays a role in inviting people into the courtyard and ultimately into the building, the mural plays a pivotal role in telling the complete narrative of the library—that inclusion wasn't always standard practice. It's a stark reminder that it takes the bravery of a few to stand against injustice on behalf of the many.

3. *Work to connect diverse local cultures.*

We wanted to ensure that we celebrated the ethnic, racial, and socioeconomic diversity of the city. One key way that we accomplished this was through a renewed effort to diversify our book collection. Doing so helped us to respond to local culture and reflect the unique interests of the community. We worked not only to find

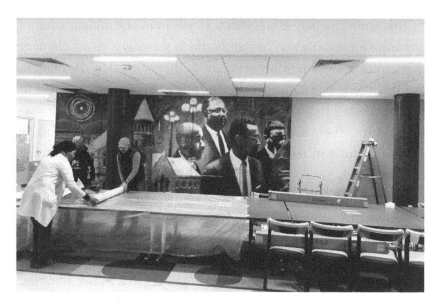

Artist Anthony Lee installs a mural on the first floor of Cossitt Library. (Source: Shamichael Hallman)

Grand reopening ceremony for Cossitt Library in 2023, with the completed mural in the background. (Source: Shamichael Hallman)

books that celebrate the rich history of Memphis and of Cossitt Library, but also to celebrate what was currently happening in the city. We believed that it was important for people to see themselves— and others—in the books. In our displays, we worked to highlight Black emo, goth, and scene culture in response to input from the community. We added books to the collection after pulling in suggestions from organizations such as We Need Diverse Books and the Black Caucus American Library Association, local nonprofits such OUTMemphis (a 501(c)(3)–certified nonprofit organization that empowers, connects, educates, and advocates for the LGBTQ+ community of the Mid-South), and local professors whose research was centered on Native American and Indigenous studies. Doing so allowed us to have one more touch point in both inviting new audiences and also educating library patrons to new cultures and worlds.

Another way that we highlight local cultures and attract members from across the community is through the power of festivals and performances.

4. Hire a diverse staff that reflects the community, and create new models to work with local talent.

In addition to having a staff that reflects the community, we saw the need for staff members who could cultivate relationships in the community, develop innovative community programs and workshops, and coordinate diverse partnerships. As often as we could, we looked to fill available roles with individuals who had a master's degree in library and information science, ideally with a specialization in user services and community engagement, data curation and services, or children and youth services. However, it was often difficult to find people in the community with this specific experience. So we created a position of library programming specialist, which opened up an opportunity for candidates who had a wide range of skills and degrees in areas such as computer

An outdoor festival featuring Black women artists on the grounds of Cossitt Library. (Source: Shamichael Hallman)

Community organizers host a "human chess" tournament on the grounds of Cossitt Library. (Source: Shamichael Hallman)

science, education, and business. While these individuals could work in many other environments, often for much more pay, candidates were drawn to the ideas and values embodied by the library. Having a mix of established librarians working alongside the new staff members paid big dividends for the library in bringing in new perspectives that reflect more of the community.

In addition to diversifying the full- and part-time staff, we explored ways of bringing in community talent. One model that worked exceptionally well was the Innovator-in-Residence (IiR). Taken from a highly successful model that we discovered while visiting the Toronto Public Library in 2018, the Innovator-in-Residence program at Cossitt Library provided an opportunity for an experienced professional to connect with and to support learners with an interest in a particular topic. The role of the IiR was to facilitate workshops, offer a limited number of one-to-one sessions with the public, host lectures, create training opportunities for library staff, and spark meaningful interactions with library patrons. Cossitt Library's first IiR was Ena Esco, a twenty-plus-year radio veteran who had worked in various roles, such as producer, voice-over talent, morning show cohost, and midday and weekend talent.

The IiRs generally serve a three- to four-month stint in the library. The library will then break for some period of time—say, another three months—and then start the process again with a new IiR who specializes in some other area (textiles, photography, business, etc.).

5. *Research and pilot a variety of programs intended to achieve the stated goals of the library.*

Library programming—proactive, intentional activities developed to meet the needs and interests of an anticipated target

Members of the Cossitt Library staff as featured in a 2021 issue of *Smithsonian Magazine*. (Source: Ariel Cobbert)

audience—was an area where we placed a great deal of focus. Aside from improvements to the physical structure, programs are one of the public library's greatest tools in serving communities. First and foremost, library programs provide a vehicle by which you can bring people in proximity with one another to experience something together—the joy of discussing a highly acclaimed book, the awe of experiencing the art or food of another culture, or the fun in playing a game with a friend or stranger. Programs can reach a wide range of individuals, including kids, teens, and adults. Memphis Public Libraries had already been recognized nationally for providing library programs that met a wide range of community interest and needs and were deployed in innovative ways. As a team, we wanted to make sure to build on that success.

Creating a list of exciting programming meant that we needed to start with the end in mind, and that involved answering two key questions: "Whom do we aim to attract?" and "What is the desired outcome of the program?"

Although some of our programs were designed for the broad public, others were designed to serve a particular group, often one that had been underserved by other institutions or systems. And while every program would have a slightly different outcome, depending on the audience, there were two overarching goals for programs: (1) respond to the needs and desires of the community; and (2) foster a sense of belonging. With these two goals in mind, we piloted a variety of programs.

Early in the process, our research led us to a helpful article in *Library Quarterly*. "Categorizing Library Public Programs," written by Jena Barchas-Lichtenstein and others, presents a framework for characterizing public programs offered by US libraries as well as seven intended programmatic outcomes.[8] The first outcome is that *participants learn new knowledge*. The next outcome is that *participants learn a new skill*. We knew that we would excel at both of these with the work we were doing to add new books and resources and with the inclusion of new spaces and equipment for things such as recording and collaborating. The third outcome centered on participants *changing their attitudes* and the fourth on *changed behavior*. We worked with financial professionals to offer classes on budgeting and saving in which we encouraged people to consider opening a savings account for the first time. We also brought in a nutritionist who used books in our collection to show participants how to quickly prepare and preserve healthy food items so that these participants might live healthier lives. The goal of the next outcome centered on ensuring that *participants gain awareness of library resources, services, and/or programs*. We knew that we could incorporate this outcome into much, if not all, of our outreach efforts. One of the more ambitious efforts was called #SwingVoteMemphis; an interactive art installation that encouraged people to vote in an upcoming election while also introducing them to a resource on our website called Informed Voter that provided key information about voter registration, polling locations, and information about candidates for upcoming elections. We often heard from citizens that they had had no idea the library offered such a resource.

The sixth outcome centered on *participants having fun or being exposed to something new such as art or food*, and again this was a really great way for us to be able to introduce people to a topic and then, by checking out our curated list of books, continue to learn about that topic. To achieve this outcome we focused on programs such as recipe swaps, "how to" festivals, and "paint 'n' sip" events that took advantage of the unobstructed view of the Mississippi

Swing Vote Memphis, a playful art installation, was part of a civic engagement campaign of Memphis Public Libraries. (Source: Shamichael Hallman)

from our back lawn. The last outcome sought to ensure that *participants met or engaged in dialogue with people that they would not have met otherwise*—which was a phrase that seemed to bubble up in nearly everything that we did. We found many ways to achieve this goal. One summer, during the renovation of the building, we hosted an outdoor music series over a period of four weeks, as mentioned in the introduction of the book. This series was a key part of our summer programming strategy. Each week featured an artist from a different genre, and the performance was offered completely free to the community. Midway through the performance we would ask the artist to create a "meet and greet" moment where the people in the audience were encouraged to meet someone new.

The series provided wonderful opportunities for conversation and bonding and added a relatively light touch to an existing program. In other cases, we worked to create programs that were designed specifically to spark conversations around weightier topics. One such event was called CitizenFEST Memphis, a free festive learning summit on how to exercise civic power, hosted by the library in partnership with Citizen University. Activists, artists, and everyday citizens were invited to come together for a unique blend of art, creativity, and lessons on the concrete skills of effective change-making. During the half-day session conversation topics included:

- "Do They Still Matter? The Role of Community Anchors"
- "Can They Bridge the Divide: Arts as a Healing Mechanism for a City"
- "Are You Next? Running for an Elected Position"

CitizenFEST Memphis drew nearly a hundred people from zip codes across Memphis and beyond. Extra care was taken to ensure that a diversity of thought was in the room, and that grounding rules were put in place so that diverse opinions could be shared safely. The event was so successful that we launched a series of shorter versions in various libraries and college campuses across the city.

Altogether, we created sixty programs to pilot. While we ultimately didn't test all of them, the ones that we launched did accomplish our goals. Those programs include:

- Civic Saturday—a civic analogue to a faith gathering. Civic Saturday brings friends and strangers together to nurture a spirit of shared purpose.
- Find Your Voice—an introduction to all things podcasting.
- How to Stage a Protest—a series of sit-downs that fostered intergenerational dialogue between high school students and civil rights protestors, resulting in the high school students using the arts to create new forms of protest.

In collaboration with Citizen University, Memphis Public Libraries host Citizen-FEST Memphis, a festive summit on civic power. (Source: Citizen University)

- Jeghetto Puppet Spring Residency and FLASH MOB Parade—a series of educational performances and workshops that used puppetry and other artistic media, including spoken word, music, and projections, to teach social justice concepts to young people.
- Smartphone Photography 101—an introductory skills workshop that exposed young and older adults to the beauty around them in the city of Memphis and ways of using that as inspiration for creating beautiful images from everyday life.
- Any Book Club: Memphis Edition—a book club that featured books by Memphis authors.
- Riverfront Storytime—an interactive story time and puppet show that incorporated elements and stories highlighting various bodies of water, including the Mississippi River.

Families take part in an outdoor story-time event at Cossitt Library in Memphis. (Source: Shamichael Hallman)

It is a winning formula that we have used time and time again. The achievements include a 227 percent increase in the number of items checked out and the total number of minutes of reading time spent by teens during the summer reading program, an 11 percent increase in the number of digital materials checked out (totaling 443,821), and a significant increase in program attendance—both virtually and in person—across the entire library system.[9]

Beyond the Memphis Public Library

While the Memphis story is unique in that we were given the opportunity, through a renovation effort, to start from scratch, we drew ideas and inspiration from other libraries. One such story is that of the Chicago Public Library, which members of the Memphis Public Library's leadership team visited over a seven-year span starting in 2009.

Under the guidance of Jennifer Lizak, coordinator of special projects in the Adult Services Department, the Chicago Public Library (CPL) has embarked on an ambitious cultural initiative called Culture in My Neighborhood (CiMN) that is redefining the library's role in the city. This initiative, rooted in equity, accessibility, and community engagement, is working to extend the library's reach beyond its traditional boundaries, offering a variety of programs that reflect and celebrate the city's diverse cultural landscape. From engaging author talks and community-driven art projects to innovative partnerships with cultural institutions like the Art Institute of Chicago, CPL is not just serving its community—it's actively enriching it, making culture accessible to all corners of the city. Through strategic planning, a commitment to inclusivity, and an understanding of the profound impact of shared cultural experience to highlight communities, CPL's initiative is a testament to the power of libraries to serve as catalysts for community development, social cohesion, and cultural enrichment. The Chicago Public Library is transforming the narrative of what a library can be and do, fostering a sense of belonging and pride among Chicagoans and setting a new standard for libraries around the world.

Their CiMN initiative emphasizes equitable access to arts and culture citywide, leveraging CPL's extensive network of eighty-one locations to host a wide array of programs. As Jennifer Lizak stated,

Everyone deserves to see a great concert in their neighborhood, no matter what neighborhood they're in. Everyone also deserves to be able to participate in a workshop or to take a walking tour celebrating their neighborhood or to create a mural with their neighbors. . . . What really brings communities together and builds communities is having those experiences together with your neighbors. And those so often happen in the realm of the arts and the culture and kind of fun types of interactive experiences like that. So that's why we thought it was important.

CPL's programs range from concerts and art workshops to walking tours and drag queen story time, aiming to reflect and serve the community's diverse interests and backgrounds. The goal is not only to provide free and accessible cultural programming but also to foster community engagement, understanding, and exploration across different cultures and neighborhoods. Speaking specifically of the walking tours, Jennifer went on to state:

> And so these neighborhood walking tours have been really popular for many years, and we take different kinds of approaches with them, like public art in this neighborhood or a small-business approach in this neighborhood. One of the quotes that I thought really made me feel great was somebody was like, "I love going to the walking tours. It helps me explore neighborhoods I've never been to, and then I spend time in them." And I think that that's an example of what we're trying to do to help people make those connections in their own city to places they've never been before, and then be able to spend more time in those different places that they've never explored.

One notable aspect of CPL's approach is its unwavering commitment to equity and accessibility in cultural programming. Leveraging its extensive network across the city, CPL ensures that high-quality cultural experiences are accessible to all neighborhoods, particularly those that are underserved. This inclusive strategy democratizes culture, transcending socioeconomic barriers and geographic divides. By addressing issues of segregation and economic inequality, CPL is striving to offer cultural enrichment opportunities to all residents, regardless of background or location.

CHAPTER 6

Looking Ahead

Envisioning futures is a core role of urban composition.
Built forms have frequently endured long past their initial
purposes, builders, or even civilizations, and our built com-
positions will be transformed by continuing urbanization,
aging populations, migrations, and other consequences of
climate change, automation, the continued evolution of virtual worlds . . . and other emerging and unseen trends. Understanding how these forces may (re)shape public spaces is
critical to (re)composing spaces that will serve us well during
their long lives.
—Mark C. Childs, "What If? Forecasting and
Composing Public Spaces"

WHAT DOES THE FUTURE HOLD for public libraries? In what
new ways might we need the library to show up, and how might
we support the library and cultivate it together? And at a time

when democracy is under siege and citizens struggle to transcend polarization, some Americans are seeking new ways to address the daunting issues dividing the country. Libraries are proving to be a pivotal part of the solution. As has been noted throughout this book, many library professionals are stepping up and becoming "Agents of Civic Awakening" (a term coined by Harry C. Boyte) through efforts to bridge political divides, inspire community service, and close gaps in civic learning—something our country desperately needs. And yet numerous opportunities continue to unfold for libraries to more fully embrace civic literacy as central to their instructional programs, and for civic learning advocates who have not yet recognized the important role that libraries can play in advancing common concerns. As noted by Nancy Kranich in her article "Civic Literacy: Reimagining a Role for Libraries" in *Library Quarterly*: "Civic literacy must become a higher national priority if we are to prepare good citizens to participate actively in our democracy . . . and libraries can play key roles through efforts such as launching a 'National Forum on Civic Literacy,' and expanding opportunities for lifelong civic learning."[1]

It is also likely that the importance of creating welcoming and inclusive spaces will grow in a society that is becoming more diverse. Yet an aging population, the pace of technological innovation, income inequality, an increase in climate-related disasters, the digital divide, and the growing economic divide will continue to create challenges for public libraries to create truly inclusive spaces and meet the growing needs of the communities they serve.

It is clear that traditional notions of public libraries simply no longer fit. The examples in this book offer just a glimpse into the increased role of the public library in response to community needs. Numerous examples exist of libraries large and small, urban, suburban, and rural, that are finding new and innovative ways of meeting changing demands and needs of the communities they serve. Take for instance the James C. Poole Memorial Library in Eutaw, Alabama. With Eutaw's population of just under three thousand, of which nearly 29 percent lives below the poverty line, the public library serves as a lifeline and critical community resource. The library partners with organizations such as Family Guidance Center of Alabama (Kids and Kin) and Project Rebound. The free Kids and Kin program has been designed to meet the needs of relative childcare providers and to raise their level of awareness about the importance of their roles. Educational workshops, resources, and a quarterly provider newsletter are just some of the resources offered to relative care providers. For instance, a Kids and Kin program called "What's Love Got to Do With It? Helping Children Thrive in a Confusing World," hosted at the library in October of 2023, highlighted increasing rates of mental illness and thoughts of suicide in children and teens—and sought to equip caregivers with the skills to help kids thrive. The Kids and Kin program also offers a voluntary certification program through which providers earn health and safety items, books, and learning materials for attending free training sessions related to childcare. Project Rebound is a resource for tornado victims, providing help with whatever needs they might have, said Teresa Lien, supervisor for the federal program created after Hurricane Ivan. (Alabama experienced the second-highest number of tornados in the state's history in 2022.)[2] The library also offered a program called "How to Manage Stress after Disaster."

Welcoming All in a Changing World

As I have covered in this book, the focus on antiracism, digital equity, and inclusion has been steadily growing within public libraries. Efforts and programs aimed at these areas are actively tackling structural racism, systemic inequity, and social injustices within the library and throughout the community. These initiatives include integrating antiracism, equity, diversity, and inclusion into strategic planning, organizing to achieve antiracist outcomes, conducting audits of library operations for antiracist practices, fostering community engagement through partnerships and discussions of systemic racism and social justice, as well as collaborating to provide high-speed broadband access to all households and promote community-wide digital literacy. In my time at the Memphis Public Library, I spent some time exploring the strategic plans of public libraries of all sizes. This strategic planning tool, when used correctly, gives public libraries a look into the communities they serve and offers new insights, challenges, partnership opportunities, and areas to innovate. I engaged in this research more deeply for purposes of this book—to get a sense of not just where libraries are, but where they may be heading.

The words *access* and *inclusion* were found in virtually every strategic plan I studied. The terms *innovation* and *adaptability* were used frequently. Historically, libraries have democratized knowledge, acting as neighborhood anchors where individuals engage with diverse ideas, and promoting education and lifelong learning. Ensuring equitable access to information—regardless of origin, age, background, or views, is a core library principle, contributing to a fairer society.

Achieving this goal involves a series of strategic efforts aimed at creating environments where every individual feels welcomed, represented, and supported, transcending backgrounds, abilities, and circumstances. Part of creating an inclusive and welcoming environment means improving physical accessibility to library facilities to ensure that individuals with disabilities can access and enjoy library services without barriers.

Some of the most innovative programs look to meet community members where they are (including people in the community who are unhoused), address growing health disparities and increased mental health challenges, expand support for workforce development, and bridge the digital divide.

Beyond the Bookmobile: Meeting Community Members Where They Are

Many of the programs presented in this book are focused on welcoming people into the library. But there are other ways to bring the support and connection offered by a library community to people who do not want to or cannot come to a physical building.

One example is the San Jose Public Library (SJPL) #RightToLibrary program that was launched in 2017. Located in the heart of Silicon Valley, San Jose is the twelfth largest city in the nation, and 40 percent of its population is foreign-born. #RightToLibrary maintains that everyone, no matter their race, age, gender, religion, sexuality, and immigration status, has the right to access knowledge, opportunities, and information.

In addition to the main San Jose library, which is a collaborative effort with San Jose State University, SJPL boasts twenty-four branches across the city. Despite this extensive network, they recognize that not every neighborhood has convenient access to a physical library. To bridge this gap, they established "bridge libraries" in partnership with local organizations. These libraries, strategically located in underserved areas, offer collections of materials and information about the public library, providing residents with closer access to books and resources. Further engaging the community,

SJPL hosts programs at these locations to encourage library sign-ups and introduce newcomers to the concept of libraries, especially those newcomers who may be unfamiliar with library services due to being new to the country. They tailor programming to cater to diverse audiences, ensuring that individuals browsing these collections receive guidance from staff on understanding the offerings of the public library system. Their materials are translated into the languages spoken most frequently in the city, including Spanish, Vietnamese, and Chinese. They acknowledge the need for additional translations, and strive to maintain accessibility by ensuring that their website is consistently available in these languages.

In Mesa County, Colorado, Words on Wheels is a service for patrons who are not able to get to the library. On a biweekly basis, the Words on Wheels van stops at more than thirty different locations, including many assisted-living and retirement homes. The service delivers fiction and nonfiction books, large-print books, audiobooks, magazines, and movies. The service is available to individuals and groups of all ages, as well as those with disabilities, extended illnesses, or any other type of condition that makes it physically impossible to enjoy the benefits that the library has to offer.

In Massachusetts, the Cambridge Public Library has invested in robust programming and services for elders and others who may be homebound, according to library director Maria McCauley. "So," she explains, "we have a senior services librarian who coordinates a book club with a senior housing development in Cambridge. And we have all kinds of programs that are done mostly by the adult services team. They offer anything from a solo aging series to an aging in place series—those are in partnership with Cambridge nonprofits. They are really popular."

For older adults who are able to travel to the library, there are exercise classes and a series called Creative Aging that aims to foster community and provide avenues for engagement between folks who are age fifty-five and above.

In New York, the Brooklyn Public Library reopened the Sunset Park branch in 2023, co-located with affordable housing units. With only 7,500 square feet available to the public before the renovation, the branch was packed to capacity and also in desperate need of renovation. The library renovation incurred costs of $17 million, approximately half of the usual expense for a comparable project, while the residential component amounted to $36.7 million. This type of solution is yet another way in which libraries are finding creative ways to meet the growing needs of the community.[3]

Health and Wellness

Understanding that Pacific Islanders and Latinx people have some of the highest rates of diabetes, hypertension, and heart disease in the state, the Salt Lake County Library system built a new library in the Kerns community—where populations of both groups reside—designed to be a community center providing information, classes, and resources to encourage changes in eating and exercise habits to improve health outcomes for all citizens. In 2022 the library system, in partnership with five community organizations, reached more than 200,000 people with health information, had 300 people sign up for diabetes prevention and management programs, and the blood-pressure cuffs were checked out nearly 100 times.[4]

In New York City, a collaboration of the New York Public Library, Columbia University, and the National Black Leadership Commission on Health created ten short animated videos on topics such as mental wellness and its benefits, monitoring stress, self-care, person-to-person comfort, and getting professional help. Each video was released online in both English and Spanish and featured dialects specific to the most impacted communities, so that the translations would feel authentic to people in the neighborhoods that the project aimed to reach.

The Alameda County Library in the Bay Area of California held a five-month initiative to increase health awareness at a time when they were not doing in-person programming due to the pandemic. Dubbed Health Challenge 2022, the program featured five key facets of health literacy: financial, social, physical, spiritual, and mental. Residents were encouraged to complete activities to qualify for prizes. Checklists capture the best practices to achieve different facets of health and encourage learning about practices from different cultures. The library system had an impressive response, with 551 entries.

Workforce Development and Skill-Building

Programs that promote economic mobility and opportunity and support entrepreneurship and workforce development are a growing area of focus for public libraries. Programs enable entrepreneurs to move forward without a significant upfront investment, in environments that are affirming and supportive of the unique needs of their community. Free and low-cost resources are particularly advantageous for individuals historically underrepresented in entrepreneurship and those lacking the financial means to pursue formal training programs. Developing a business plan, identifying potential customers, finding funding sources, and being part of a community of like-minded individuals sharing an interest in small business are some of the most sought-after goals according to the 2022 report *Entrepreneurship: Where Urban Libraries Fit.*[5] The report highlights a number of case studies that demonstrated that a "wide range of entrepreneurs rely on urban libraries for support, including freelance craftsmen, students, adults in career transition, and some individuals running larger enterprises."

One example, which would also fit with the goal of meeting people where they are, is the Los Angeles Public Library (LAPL) mobile program for street vendors to learn business, digital, and English-language skills. The library system worked with Cell-Ed, a digital learning and coaching platform, to build micro-lessons that vendors could complete on a mobile phone. Lessons include basic Internet skills; business, sales, vending, and community safety. Street vendors in Los Angeles are often excluded from resources because of their limited access to and understanding of the formal systems required to operate legal businesses. The prerequisites for becoming a proprietor are both new and intricate, presenting a challenge for many vendors, particularly those who are not English speakers and/or have limited literacy skills. Through this unique program, more than 100 individuals enrolled in the courses and cited such key lessons learned as "better understanding of managing expenses and tracking cash flow."

Other noteworthy initiatives include Rock It! Lab, a partnership between Central Arkansas Library System and Advancing Black Entrepreneurship, which is working to remove barriers that under-resourced entrepreneurs, including African Americans, Latinx people, women, and veterans face when seeking resources and support. Rock It! Lab offers a variety of educational programs, retail and coworking space, and access to knowledge, mentorship, and capital. In 2021, the program delivered 115 entrepreneur consultations, engaged more than 300 participants in its various programs, hosted 15 vendors, and had just under 120 applicants for a new incubator program.

A number of library programs work to center the needs of local workers and job-seekers. In 2023, the San Diego Public Library initiated a quarterly workforce development program aimed at training young adults aged sixteen to thirty in filmmaking. Following their completion of the six-week training program, students transition into a paid internship at various branches, where they produce videos highlighting library programs, capturing patron stories, and narrating the library's own story. Throughout their training, interns receive a stipend, transit passes, and a clothing allowance. The culmination of the internship program is marked by a red-carpet event, resembling a film festival, where the documentaries created by the interns are screened. According to the latest cohort survey, 92 percent of interns have acquired new skills, while 100 percent have reported successfully completing tasks they couldn't do previously or couldn't do as effectively.

Public libraries prioritize education and learning, serving as vital hubs that enhance access to high-quality learning opportunities for people of all ages. These initiatives are designed to advance personal and family learning objectives while fostering literacy in different areas. They encompass partnerships with K–12 school leaders and local organizations to promote education and community engagement. Additionally, libraries offer diverse programs such as summer learning experiences, youth mentorship, internships, and leadership development initiatives. They also provide trauma-informed programming, caregiver workshops, and learning circles to address specific needs within the community.

The Prince William Public Libraries (PWPL) in Virginia serve a community where over fifty thousand adults lack a high school diploma, per the 2020 Census. PWPL recognized the scarcity of avenues for these individuals to enhance their skills, which limits their ability to earn a living and potentially to further their education. In response to this challenge, PWPL launched a flexible and supportive online program offering high school diploma and career certifications. Utilizing its year-end budget, PWPL procured twenty scholarships and awarded them to deserving adult learners.

Rounding out the list of programs focused on education is an initiative of the Dallas Public Library (DPL) system. DPL offers an array of educational programs, including a music initiative born from the dedication of a single staff member to community service and music. Originating with just three keyboards and four students, this initiative blossomed into the Music Equity Program, thanks to a grant from the state library commission. Designed to provide access to music education for residents in underserved, predominantly minority neighborhoods, the program allows participants to borrow instruments like library books, provides them with a curriculum book, and offers tailored instruction suited to their skill levels. Initially confined to two library branches, the program expanded, hosting seasonal recitals to showcase students' progress. In spring 2022, classes were held at three library locations, delivering seventy-seven sessions to more than four hundred eager learners.

Digital Equity

In Nevada, the Las Vegas–Clark County Library District (LVCCLD) initiated a program to assist vulnerable residents, particularly those experiencing homelessness who rely on mobile devices to stay connected to friends, families, and essential services. Through collaboration with the NV Homeless Alliance, NV Partnership for Homeless Youth, and Premier Wireless, LVCCLD launched a Cell Phone Lending program. This initiative provided Internet connectivity to 435 at-risk adults and teens. The phones distributed were preloaded with contacts for social and employment services, as well as community and library educational resources. Pre-screened clients were invited to an event featuring one-on-one tutorials, a vendor fair with social service providers, library card sign-ups, immunizations, and access to a mobile shower truck. Following an eighteen-month complimentary period, clients have the option to retain their phone and number, continuing service at their own expense.

The San Francisco Public Library, in collaboration with the Friends of San Francisco Public Library, initiated a program aimed at bridging the digital gap by empowering individuals with the necessary tools and skills to navigate the digital landscape effectively. Donated laptops were refurbished and provided to people in the community along with a comprehensive multi-week training course. Upon completion of the training cycle, participants received fully functional laptop computers. In addition to having the proficiency to use the laptops, they were provided with information about broadband subsidies and accessing library services online. The four-week course was available in Spanish, Mandarin, and English. The effort redistributed forty-seven laptops to community members, which kept them out of landfills. The impact of this initiative was transformative, as evidenced by participant testimonials expressing gratitude and newfound opportunities. "It will help me get trained so I can be more useful and maybe get a job," wrote one participant. "I have never had a computer before. I cannot believe this is happening to me," wrote another.

In Texas, the Frisco Public Library offers the use of a Rocky AI robot maker kit. Patrons can either write code in Python or use a visual code editor with drag-and-drop coding to create the software that controls the robot. This involves working with artificial intelligence and deep-learning engines. Through this kit, users learn coding skills and machine-learning techniques, as well as voice and image recognition.

For those aged eighteen and above, there's also a Google AIY Voice smart speaker available. This allows for learning about artificial intelligence and using Python coding skills to customize and enhance the existing artificial intelligence functionalities. Google's AIY ("do-it-yourself artificial intelligence") transforms powerful AI technology into a cardboard box, opening up countless possibilities. These kits require some software installation and connection to motors or lights for control purposes.

The Reading Public Library in Pennsylvania recently added the Oculus Quest 2 Virtual Reality Kit to its collection. The Oculus Quest 2 is a headset designed for users to immerse themselves in the virtual world. Equipped with various programs, users can engage in a plethora of activities, including playing games, exploring the International Space Station through Mission: ISS: Quest, participating in fitness routines such as FitXR, Boxing, HIIT, and dance workouts, experiencing thrilling roller coaster rides, and much more.

A Library of Things

A library of things, also known as a tool library or lending library, is becoming a popular community resource at public libraries. The libraries make available for loan tools of everyday life such as power tools, kitchen appliances, camping gear, sports equipment, board games, musical instruments, and more.

In an interview on the *Ezra Klein Show*, Emily Drabinksi, president of the American Library Association, talked about what this type of program can mean to the community. "I was in Des Moines, Iowa, touring a library. And they have a library of things, which many, many public libraries have these days. And they circulate book club kits and sensory kits for kids and science materials and cake pans and tools.

"And this library had started circulating two carpet-cleaning machines. And I remember growing up in Boise, Idaho, my mother saving up for months to be able to rent that carpet cleaner at the

Albertsons in Boise so she could clean our carpets. And this library takes that out of the equation. And it means everybody can clean their carpet. And it seems like a small thing. It's one thing happening in Des Moines, Iowa, but multiply that by the hundreds and thousands of public libraries across the country, and every single one of them has something like that that's securing and expanding access to public resources for everyone."[6]

In Ohio, the Hubbard Public Library has introduced a Toy Lending Library, which offers exciting opportunities for hands-on learning with educational toys including a doll house, a musical llama, family games such as Zingo, SmartGames that facilitate problem-solving skills, and "Sprout Early Learning Backpacks" filled with books, educational toys, and games. The Stark County Library offers access to air-quality monitors, electricity usage meters, and even vehicle diagnostic-code readers.

The Arlington Public Library in Virginia has a DIY collection that encompasses both traditional and nontraditional hand tools such as screwdrivers, levels, and stud finders, as well as garden tools such as tree pruners, hedge sheers, and bulb planters. The City of Nevada Library in Iowa has in its collection an Orion SkyQuest XT8 Dobsonian Reflector telescope.

In Maryland, the Carroll County Library offers access to fishing poles, knitting needles, and rubber stamps. The Framingham Public Library offers an array of kitchen equipment including cake-decorating kits, food dehydrators, kitchen scales, and even a KitchenAid juicer and pasta-making attachments.

Building Support

One of my proudest moments was the day that Cossitt Library in Memphis finally reopened to the public in 2023. As library staff gave tours of the building, you could see how much pride and excitement reverberated throughout the building. This building, once in threat of being torn down, had been reimagined with the community into an invaluable local resource. Artists and arts-related organizations begin planning the types of events and programs they would host. Community groups began booking the meeting room spaces months out. Individuals who were interested in creative hobbies such as podcasting, filmmaking, and sewing started to look at the equipment offerings that we had and signed up for classes. Local authors inquired about hosting book signings and talks. In the year that followed, a number of high-profile events have occurred at the branch. All of this speaks to the power of how well-designed, high-quality civic assets can generate excitement and instill a sense of pride in a community.

A photography festival at Cossitt Library in Memphis. (Source: Ariel Cobbert)

While the offerings of libraries are tailored to the communities they serve, there are seven general benefits of libraries:

1. Public libraries are welcoming and inviting places that can be accessed by all regardless of socioeconomic status, political ideology, or physical condition. In a world where goods and services are increasingly becoming privatized, libraries stand as an example of a public good that can be shared by all. As such, they create opportunities for interactions and encounters among people from different parts of a community. Sometimes these interactions are brief and short-lived, and other times they are long-term. Both types of interactions are highly beneficial for society and can lead to new relationships and experiences. Places that are accessible to all ensure that amenities can be enjoyed by all. Whether you have a comfortable financial situation or you don't have a dollar to your name, the public library is the same.

2. Public libraries are the place to become a better version of yourself. In an age where self-help gurus and courses flood the Internet, the library offers a prime space in which you can launch a new business, champion a cause, or learn a new hobby. Additionally, because you are in a public setting you have the option to go at it alone, or you can find a community of people who are also passionate and interested in similar topics.

3. Public libraries are protectors of privacy. Every American should care about who has access to their personal information and what is being done with it. Whether you are researching how to get started with a new hobby or are working through personal challenges, struggles, or identity, you can be assured that whatever activity you engage in at a public library is private and protected. This is what is meant, in

part, by intellectual freedom and privacy. Intellectual privacy encompasses the right to explore ideas, form opinions, and engage in intellectual pursuits without scrutiny. Such a level of privacy ensures that individuals can explore diverse viewpoints, controversial topics, and sensitive materials without fear of judgment or reprisal.

Libraries have a long history of resisting censorship and surveillance, advocating for individuals' rights to access information freely.

4. Public libraries are the promoters of a circular economy: a model of production and consumption that involves sharing, leasing, reusing, repairing, refurbishing, and recycling materials and products whenever possible. This concept is the foundation of the sharing economy. Libraries have consistently led the way in showcasing the worth and possibilities of freely accessible resources and communal spaces. With the evolution of the sharing economy into various sectors like electronic devices, transportation, tools, education, and equipment, libraries are already adjusting and evolving their roles as facilitators of sharing. Additionally, libraries sometimes facilitate book swaps or borrowing programs where community members can exchange or borrow books instead of purchasing new ones.

5. Public libraries are pillars of reliable information. At this moment in our country's history, there is perhaps no greater need than reliable factual information, and no greater source than the public library in providing the general population with media and digital literacy skills. This touches on two terms that you have probably heard: misinformation and disinformation. *Misinformation* refers to false or inaccurate information that is spread without malice. Misinformation can be generated due to misunderstandings, mistakes, or

misinterpretations about a topic. *Disinformation*, on the other hand, is spread with the intent to deceive or manipulate others. It involves the deliberate creation and dissemination of false information, often for political, ideological, or malicious reasons. Public libraries develop and offer information literacy programs to educate patrons on how to critically evaluate sources, fact-check information, and discern credible sources from unreliable ones.

6. Public libraries serve as pathfinders, often serving as the first stop for individuals looking for resources in a community. They play a crucial role in empowering individuals with the knowledge and information they need to make informed decisions. Librarians regularly curate collections of books, pamphlets, and online resources focused on topics such as medical care, homebuying, and legal aid.

7. Public libraries are partner-centered institutions that very often amplify the initiatives of other institutions. In areas such as education, workforce and entrepreneurship, and mental and physical health, libraries are the go-to and preferred partner of many organizations. As such, you will often see libraries play a key role in the overall health and prosperity of your community.

These seven benefits to communities aren't always top of mind when people think about libraries, yet they should be. My hope is that, by reading this book, you have gained a new understanding and appreciation for this treasured resource that exists in our communities. As libraries work to reimagine themselves, it is equally important for communities to move beyond dated ideas of what the library stands for and does on a daily basis. Make no mistake about it, this requires more work on the part of public libraries. A continuous dialogue between the library and society can help to bridge the gap between misconceptions and reality—while also increasing the visibility, awareness, and use of a library's offerings and services. All of this must happen as the libraries work to continually reimagine themselves and offer new and innovative services and programs—all while targeting new audiences and using new media to do so. The library is a lifeline for many in our society, providing essential access to knowledge and information, Internet access, socialization, and in some cases even shelter (much to the displeasure and disapproval of some). At the local library you can register to vote, learn to read, apply for benefits, become competent in a new skill, or launch your next great venture. A library is a safe space for kids after school, a cool spot during a warm day, and a warm place to escape the cold months. It's a place to learn, whether you have a GED, a PhD, or no degree at all. This is the reimagined library.

But the reimagining of libraries also requires those outside the profession to imagine anew the role of libraries and library workers. The dated idea of the library as just a place for books also brings with it a dated image of librarians and library professionals. Yes, they love books as much as many other library lovers. However, it far more likely that on any given day at the library, rather than reading a book, they are helping someone find a book, apply for a job, or prepping for an upcoming event at the library.

In my current role at Urban Libraries Council I'm working to build a conversation on how public libraries in North America lead civic engagement and how this work ties directly to strengthening our democracies, informs antiracism, and leads to stronger collective community action. I also direct the organization's work to strengthen the library's role in advancing economic opportunity for under-resourced and historically disadvantaged communities, including our focus on equitable entrepreneurship. These roles have allowed me to see the great lengths to which librarians are going to not only understand the intricate needs of their

A volunteer helps disassemble a bookshelf at Cossitt Library in Memphis.
(Source: Shamichael Hallman)

communities, but also to find innovative ways to meet those needs. Librarians are in the community forging partnerships with chambers of commerce, community colleges, and faith-based organizations. They are revising existing programs in an effort to reach new audiences. Many of those drawn to the library profession have a deep desire to see communities change for the better. And they know the library is one of the organizations by which that change can happen. Librarians are doing the very hard but necessary work of addressing inequality and oppression; promoting diversity and inclusivity; and propelling racial and social justice forward within our libraries and communities. As they take on bigger roles and face opposition and backlash for the work they are doing to welcome all, we need to find ways to support libraries and library staff in their work to bridge a widening divide.

Sign up for a library card. And use it.

Be an advocate for your library by writing letters of support to your local elected officials.

Vote for candidates who support libraries.

Organize events at your local branch: a concert, a book club, a community dialogue, or whatever excites you.

Volunteer for an upcoming event.

Join your Friends of the Library group.

Take the things that I've shared in this book and spread the word about the value of the library to neighbors, friends, and decision-makers.

Libraries inspire, empower, and transform not only the people who use them but also the communities in which they are situated. Public libraries are not an artifact of the past. They are essential to the future.

Afterword

by Bridget Marquis

From Insights to Action: Your Library Can Reconnect the Nation

IF YOU HAVE READ THIS FAR, you are likely inspired to bring some of the ideas from *Meet Me at the Library* into your own work. Yet you are also probably looking for guidance about exactly *how* to do that: how does one transform a branch library or library system into something that becomes a piece of the solution for the unique forms of division, economic segregation, and social isolation that plague America today?

For the last eight years, I have had the good fortune to work with leaders and practitioners in twelve cities across the country who are answering these questions. They have been and are focused squarely on transforming shared civic infrastructure—our parks, trails, town squares, main streets, and play spaces, as well as libraries and other public gathering spaces—into places that bring social, economic, and environmental benefits to communities.

The lessons these practitioners have learned along the way provide valuable guidance for unleashing the potential of civic infrastructure—including your library.

The multifaceted benefits of robust civic infrastructure have been documented by researchers across many fields, and include things like improved health and well-being, more trust, safer communities, and more widely shared economic prosperity. Yet to realize these benefits, we must be willing to change the way we work within, and beyond, our institutions.

The development of this "new way of working" over the past eight years has solidified a set of guiding questions that can be used by anyone interested in designing, creating, and managing civic infrastructure (read: your library) to be a part of the solution to the biggest challenges of our time.

*   *   *

I offer four of these guiding questions here to ask yourself as you begin this work:

One: Are you committed to leveraging your library to connect people across diversity and strengthening democracy?

Adopting outcomes that matter for the community and the nation, and managing your institution to deliver on those outcomes, is a powerful way to ensure that the benefits of civic infrastructure are maximized. From the very start, Reimagining the Civic Commons has asked participating cities to reconsider and plan for how their collection of civic assets can deliver on four positive—and specific—outcomes that matter. The four outcomes—civic engagement, socioeconomic mixing, environmental sustainability, and value creation—serve as North Stars for the practitioners in our network, inspiring them to reconsider all aspects of their work, from design and programming to staffing and operations.

Individual city teams across our network were tasked not only with developing strategies that worked in their particular communities to achieve each outcome, but also with tracking progress toward specific outcomes through a framework of data collection.[1]

Civic infrastructure, as networks of gathering spaces that are free and open to the public, are uniquely suited to deliver on these ambitious outcomes. However, throughout this process of adopting shared outcomes and measuring progress, we learned that intentionality matters. If you and your team are not committed to these outcomes, you won't achieve them. That means incorporating outcomes into your mission statement and strategic plan. It means interrogating every program, design, and communication to ensure that outcomes are embedded throughout your operations. Finally, it means measurement of your progress, which can be done by members of your team using DIY measurement tools.[2]

Two: Are you positioning your library as best-in-class?

Underinvestment in civic infrastructure too often results in parks, libraries, and community centers unable to provide the connective tissue that binds people together across differences. As disinvestment worsens, those with the means to depart to private spaces for recreation, relaxation, and free time do so, worsening the disinvestment. Library operations can fall to the bottom of municipal budgets and libraries themselves can be seen as "nice to have" amenities, instead of critical civic infrastructure for a stronger community.

If we want diverse people to come together, it isn't going to happen if the space is unwelcoming or if the programming is average.

What we invest in together with our public dollars should aspire to be *best in class*, able to compete with other options where people spend their time. Holding public assets to high standards in design, programming, staffing, and maintenance is key to capturing those who will otherwise decamp to offerings in the private sector.

In short, your library should seek to be a compelling place and a source of joyful interaction among diversity.

Holding this high standard for libraries creates a greater potential to attract a mix of visitors across racial, geographic, and economic backgrounds—what we call "socioeconomic mixing." These seemingly casual interactions among people of diverse backgrounds is actually a powerful local economic development tool. In fact, cross-class connections have been shown in research to be a key factor in improving economic mobility for low-income children later in life.[3] With the right facilities, offerings, and programming, libraries can be powerful tools to create socioeconomic mixing that can improve the circumstances of people's lives.

While Memphis, Tennessee, remains a city starkly divided by race and income, a cross-silo effort to transform a six-block area called the Fourth Bluff, which includes Cossitt Library, a trail, and two riverfront parks adjacent to downtown and along the Mississippi River, is successfully and regularly drawing people of different backgrounds together in public space. Through world-class design alongside thoughtful staffing and programming, the Fourth Bluff has become a gathering place for a true cross section of Memphis. Visitor intercept surveys show district visitors hailing from a wide range of socioeconomic backgrounds and a geography of more than thirty-seven different Memphis-area ZIP codes.

In addition to gathering a mix of people, the Fourth Bluff sites have seen a significant increase in opportunities for impromptu interactions among visitors, nearly tripling the number of site visitors observed within conversational distance of one another. The welcoming design and programming of the Fourth Bluff is not only gathering a diverse group of Memphians together in public space, it is also encouraging them to connect—with two-thirds of site visitors reporting that they met someone for the first time while there.

Three: Are you looking beyond your walls to inform the larger system of civic infrastructure?

It takes more than a single asset or site to deliver ambitious social, environmental, and economic outcomes in your community. This means that you can't go it alone; rather than managing libraries as individual assets, you must consider how a library can be managed as part of a broader portfolio of civic assets. When it comes to civic infrastructure operating as a network, the proximity of those assets matters.

Seek out the people who manage or program nearby assets—a park around the block, a trail down the street, an adjacent community center, or any mix of close-by public spaces where people can easily walk to from your library. Start small, by working with a "coalition of the willing" of people at those assets. You don't need everyone to be on board at the beginning, but sharing early wins and credit for those wins can lead to a larger coalition and a bigger sphere of influence. Widening your perspective to work within a portfolio requires library staff to move beyond their comfort zone and collaborate with people managing other asset types, along with philanthropy, outside agencies, nonprofit organizations, and members of the community, eliminating silos and capitalizing on each entity's unique strengths.

Leadership lives in different places, so you will want to seek out the innovators who are eager to do this work in ways that address the major challenges of our times: division, isolation, and distrust. In some communities, local government will lead the work; in others, local government will follow. The important thing is to get started.

In Akron, Ohio, a small group of five people formed an initial "coalition of the willing" in 2016 to work on revitalizing public spaces in three neighborhoods that are connected by the Ohio & Erie Canalway Towpath Trail. At first, the team met monthly and worked on modest changes. In Summit Lake, a majority-Black neighborhood that had long suffered from a lack of public and private investment, the team worked with neighborhood residents to transform an overgrown and underused lakeside into a new beachhead adjacent to the location of a weekly farmer's market. This drew more and more people to Summit Lake, leading to new activities: weekly canoe and kayak tours, quilting clubs and canning classes, and a youth-employment program that stewards the space every summer, all the while bringing more organizational partners onto the team.

This locus of activity also encouraged significant public and private investment into adjacent assets, including a previously abandoned structure transformed into a new nature center (managed by the countywide parks agency Summit Metro Parks), a new loop trail around the lake (managed by the nonprofit Ohio & Erie Canalway Coalition), and a federally funded strategic neighborhood plan (developed by Akron Metropolitan Housing Authority and the City of Akron).

Today, Akron's core team is composed of dozens of organizations and neighborhood residents working together, and their influence and impact continues to grow. The civic infrastructure projects that are a part of this growing effort have attracted multimillions in investment, including a $17.5-million transformation of Lock 3 Park in downtown and a $7.5-million investment in public amenities along the North Shore of Summit Lake.

Four: Are you ready to create new value in your community?

We know that place matters for human thriving. Research shows that where you are born and where you live impacts everything from economic mobility to health outcomes and life expectancy. Inequity and place are inherently connected, with studies showing that, across the United States, homes and businesses located in majority-Black communities are consistently devalued.[4] In addition, a lack of investment in the public realm often correlates with areas of concentrated poverty—the same places that are unable to attract private investment are also denied robust civic infrastructure.

And despite civic infrastructure being inherently place-based, it often isn't invested in as a vehicle to increase value that can counter economic, racial, and social segregation. However, as we create public places that all of us want to occupy—including new and renovated libraries—demand for nearby real estate should go up, increasing its value. In places that are currently undervalued and underinvested, this increase may be a welcome change, as longtime residents can build equity through their homes and local businesses. In fast-growth markets, however, it may raise concerns that a neighborhood could be at risk of becoming unaffordable for those who currently reside there.

When civic infrastructure is reimagined and property values begin to rise, some of that value can be captured and delivered to the benefit of local residents in the forms of real estate, local business ownership, jobs, and more. To help bring about such outcomes, you must create systems specifically designed to capture value for current residents, and put those systems into place *prior* to improvements.

For example, special assessment districts apply an additional tax on properties within a defined geographic area that can be used to fund operations, maintenance, and programming of civic infrastructure, which can prioritize hiring and contracting local residents for green and clean teams, and pay local talent for programming that centers diverse cultures. Utilizing tax increment financing can capture future value for specific improvement projects, including reimagined civic infrastructure and affordable housing. Of course, these approaches work best when you are working in a cross-silo team across a variety of assets, which might include a community development organization, a community development financial institution (CDFI), and/or your local government's planning and development department.

Detroit is a city in the middle of reinvention, and in the Livernois–Six Mile neighborhood, a cross-silo, multi-organization team has been successfully demonstrating how investing in civic infrastructure can create new value for previously disinvested neighborhoods and longtime residents. Collaborative investments in civic infrastructure by city agencies, nonprofit organizations, philanthropy, and a CDFI include a new neighborhood park, a greenway, a storefront community center, and a transformed commercial streetscape. These investments have yielded a rebound in home occupancy paired with a constant homeownership rate, and a 243 percent increase in typical home values from 2015 to 2022.[5]

Many longtime residents have remained in the Livernois–Six Mile neighborhood, with the increase in real estate value building wealth through home equity for these residents.[6] In addition, city, philanthropic, and community partners intentionally recruited local Black developers for residential and commercial redevelopment and prioritized local Black-owned businesses for renewed storefronts. The neighborhood's transformation was accomplished without displacing longtime neighbors, who are now capturing the value created through a robust public realm.

Democracy scholar and advocate Danielle Allen has said: "The health of our democracy will depend upon whether we can reactivate public space as a solution to the challenges in front of us." Strategic investments can transform libraries into the critical civic infrastructure we need to connect and unite us. Our public libraries can and must be a part of the solution.

—Bridget Marquis, Director of
Reimagining the Civic Commons
www.civiccommons.us

About the Author

SHAMICHAEL HALLMAN SERVES as the Director of Civic Health and Economic Opportunity at Urban Libraries Council, an innovation and action tank of North America's leading public library systems. In this role he's working to advance conversations about public libraries as essential city and county infrastructure, including their value as physical spaces and a connector of diverse lived experiences. From 2017 to 2022, he served as the Senior Library Manager of the historic Cossitt Library (Memphis Public Libraries), tasked with overseeing the multi-million-dollar renovation of this space, which reimagined the roles that a branch library could play in the community. During his tenure with Memphis Public Libraries, the library system was awarded the 2021 National Medal for Museum and Library Science by the Institute of Museum and Library Services and was recognized as the Nation's Most Innovative Public Library by *Smithsonian Magazine* in November of 2021. His 2020 TEDx talk, "Reimagining the Public Library to Reconnect the Community," garnered international attention among librarians and social innovators.

Hallman holds an MS in Nonprofit Leadership from the University of Pennsylvania, and was a 2023 Loeb Fellow at the Graduate School of Design at Harvard University.

Notes

Introduction

1. "Established in 1905 as the first mobile library service in the nation, the Washington County Free Library Bookmobile continues the proud tradition of serving patrons who do not otherwise have access to library services." ("Bookmobile," Washington County Free Library, 2023, https://www.washcolibrary.org/bookmobile, accessed April 6, 2024.)
2. Erica Shames, "Library Patrons Trying Out Computers," *New York Times*, April 14, 1985, https://www.nytimes.com/1985/04/14/nyregion/library-patrons-trying-out-computers.html.
3. Nancy Kranich, "Libraries and Democracy Revisited," *Library Quarterly* 90, no. 2 (2020): 121–53, https://doi.org/10.1086/707670.

4. "2022 Book Bans," Unite Against Book Bans, September 20, 2023, https://uniteagainstbookbans.org/2022-book-bans/.

5. Aidan Connaughton, "Americans See Stronger Societal Conflicts than People in Other Advanced Economies," Pew Research Center, October 13, 2021, https://www.pewresearch .org/short-reads/2021/10/13/americans-see-stronger-societal -conflicts-than-people-in-other-advanced-economies/.

6. Office of the US Surgeon General, *Our Epidemic of Loneliness and Isolation: The US Surgeon General's Advisory on the Healing Effects of Social Connection and Community*, March 2023, https://www.hhs.gov/sites/default/files/surgeon-general -social-connection-advisory.pdf.

7. Ibid.

8. Maura Kelly, "How to Get Unlonely," *Harvard Public Health*, October 17, 2023, https://harvardpublichealth.org /mental-health/project-unlonely-public-health-book-tackles -loneliness-epidemic/.

9. Jessica Buechler, "The Loneliness Epidemic Persists: A Post-Pandemic Look at the State of Loneliness among U.S. Adults," The Cigna Group, https://newsroom.thecignagroup.com /loneliness-epidemic-persists-post-pandemic-look.

10. Robert D. Putnam, Lewis M. Feldstein, and Don Cohen, *Better Together: Restoring the American Community* (New York: Simon & Schuster, 2009).

11. Vikas Mehta and Danilo Palazzo, *Companion to Public Space* (London: Routledge, 2023).

Chapter 1

1. Dan Witters, "U.S. Depression Rates Reach New Highs," Gallup.com, February 7, 2024, https://news.gallup.com /poll/505745/depression-rates-reach-new-highs.aspx.

2. Office of the US Surgeon General, *Our Epidemic of Loneliness and Isolation: US Surgeon General's Advisory on the Healing Effects of Social Connection and Community*, March 2023, https://www.hhs.gov/sites/default/files/surgeon-general -social-connection-advisory.pdf.

3. Ibid.

4. Laura Silver, "What Makes Life Meaningful? Views from 17 Advanced Economies," Pew Research Center's Global Attitudes Project, November 18, 2021, https://www.pewresearch.org /global/2021/11/18/what-makes-life-meaningful-views -from-17-advanced-economies/.

5. Viji Diane Kannan and Peter J. Veazie, "US Trends in Social Isolation, Social Engagement, and Companionship— Nationally and by Age, Sex, Race/Ethnicity, Family Income, and Work Hours, 2003–2020," *SSM Population Health* (March 2023), https://pubmed.ncbi.nlm.nih.gov/36618547/.

6. Ibid.

7. "GILC Position Statement: Loneliness & Connection," Global Initiative on Loneliness and Connection, April 2022, https: //www.gilc.global/_files/ugd/410bdf_62e236db3a7146cd 9f2654877a87dbc6.pdf.

8. Ibid.

9. "Political Polarization in the American Public: How Increasing Ideological Uniformity and Partisan Antipathy Affect Politics, Compromise, and Everyday Life," Pew Research Center, June 12, 2014. https://www.pewresearch.org/politics/2014/06/12 /political-polarization-in-the-american-public/.

10. Jonathan J. Mijs and Elizabeth L. Roe, "Is America Coming Apart? Socioeconomic Segregation in Neighborhoods, Schools, Workplaces, and Social Networks, 1970–2020," *Sociology Compass* 15, no. 6 (April 7, 2021), https://doi .org/10.1111/soc4.12884.

Chapter 2

1. Eric Klinenberg, *Palaces for the People: How Social Infrastructure Can Help Fight Inequality, Polarization, and the Decline of Civic Life* (New York: Broadway Books), 2019.

2. US Office of the Surgeon General, *Our Epidemic of Loneliness and Isolation: The US Surgeon General's Advisory on the Healing Effects of Social Connection and Community*, March 2023, https://www.hhs.gov/sites/default/files/surgeon-general -social-connection-advisory.pdf.

3. Ibid.

4. Kelly-Ann Allen et al., "Belonging: A Review of Conceptual Issues, an Integrative Framework, and Directions for Future Research," *Australian Journal of Psychology* 73, no. 1 (2021): 87–102, https://doi.org/10.1080/00049530.2021.1883409.

5. Susie Wise, *Design for Belonging: How to Build Inclusion and Collaboration in Your Communities* (Emeryville, CA: Ten Speed Press), 2022.

6. US Office of the Surgeon General, *Our Epidemic of Loneliness and Isolation*.

7. Ibid.

8. Ibid.

9. Ibid.

10. "Creating a Sustainable Civic Infrastructure" (unpublished report), Strengthen Our American Republic (SOAR), 2021.

11. Learn more at: www.civiccommons.us.

12. Harry C. Boyte, "Libraries as Free Spaces: Riverview in St. Paul," *Continuum: Magazine of the University of Minnesota Libraries*, September 18, 2021, https://www.academia.edu /52765816/Libraries_as_free_spaces_Riverview_in_St_Paul.

13. "What Is Civic Health?" Carsey School of Public Policy, University of New Hampshire, (n.d.), https://carsey.unh.edu /sites/default/files/media/2023/03/local-chi-1-what-is-civic -health-print.pdf.
14. "Civic Language Guidance: Wisdom from the Field," Philanthropy for Active Civic Engagement (PACE), February 1, 2023, http://www.pacefunders.org/civic-language-guidance/.
15. Ibid.
16. "Bridgebuilding Resources Hub for Libraries." International Research & Exchanges Board (IREX), WebJunction, August 15, 2023, https://www.webjunction.org/news/webjunction /bridge-building-resource-hub.html.

Chapter 3

1. Walter Hood and Sara Zwede, "How Can We Share Space Together?" *Harvard Design Magazine* F/W 21: Publics, no. 49, 2023.
2. City of Cambridge, Massachusetts, "Cambridge Public Library Strategic Framework," 2024, https://www.cambridgema.gov /Departments/cambridgepubliclibrary/strategicplan, accessed April 8, 2024.
3. "About Us," Cambridge Public Library, https://www .cambridgema.gov/cpl/aboutus, accessed April 4, 2024.
4. "A Library That Reinforces Community + Wellness," Urban Libraries Council, (n.d.), https://www.urbanlibraries.org /innovations/a-library-the-reinforces-community-wellness.
5. Michelle Boisvenue-Fox, "Palaces for the People: Library as Community Builder," TEDx Talk, 2021, https://www .youtube.com/watch?v=GX0wiPETk2g.

6. "Libraries Transforming Communities," American Library Association, 2021, https://www.ala.org/tools/libraries transform/libraries-transforming-communities.

Chapter 4

1. "Conversation Topics," Living Room Conversations, https://livingroomconversations.org/topics/, accessed April 4, 2024.
2. Office of the US Surgeon General, *Our Epidemic of Loneliness and Isolation: US Surgeon General's Advisory on the Healing Effects of Social Connection and Community*, March 2023, https://www.hhs.gov/sites/default/files/surgeon-general-social-connection-advisory.pdf.
3. Eric Liu, *Become America: Civic Sermons on Love, Responsibility, and Democracy* (Seattle, WA: Sasquatch Books, 2019).
4. Ibid.

Chapter 5

1. "2021 National Medal for Museum and Library Service Virtual Ceremony," YouTube, August 24, 2021, https://www.youtube.com/watch?v=kArlu-RAEFc.
2. "Reimagining Historic Cossitt Library," Urban Libraries Council, 2024, https://www.urbanlibraries.org/innovations/reimagining-historic-cossitt-library.
3. "About," Reimagining the Civic Commons, July 14, 2023, https://civiccommons.us/about/.
4. "Cossitt Library," Groundswell Design, November 30, 2018, https://www.groundswelldesigngroup.com/portfolio/cossitt-library/.
5. Amanda Miller, "Investing with Intention: Socioeconomic Mixing." Reimagining the Civic Commons, August 28, 2023. https://civiccommons.us/2021/11/socioeconomic-mixing/.

6. "Cossitt future unsure amid library plans," *Commercial Appeal* (Memphis, TN), November 19, 1992, Newspapers.com, 87, https://www.newspapers.com/image/774012678/?terms =cossitt+library&match=1, accessed March 29, 2024.

7. "memphis muse | cossitt library Public Art," UrbanArt Commission, 2022, https://uacmem.org/projects/cossitt.

8. Jena Barchas-Lichtenstein et al., "Categorizing Library Public Programs," *Library Quarterly* 90, no. 4 (October 1, 2020): 563–79, https://doi.org/10.1086/710259.

9. "MPL by the Numbers," Memphis Public Libraries, February 2, 2024, https://www.memphislibrary.org/about /mpl-by-the-numbers/.

Chapter 6

1. Nancy Kranich, "Civic Literacy: Reimagining a Role for Libraries." *Library Quarterly* 94, no. 1 (January 2024): 4–25.

2. "Alabama Tornado Occurrences, 1950–2023," National Weather Service, 2023, https://www.weather.gov/bmx /tornadostats2.

3. "The New Sunset Park Library," Brooklyn Public Library, 2024, https://www.bklynlibrary.org/locations/sunset-park /reconstruct.

4. "Community Wellness Liaisons," Urban Libraries Council, https://www.urbanlibraries.org/innovations/community -wellness-liaisons-1, accessed April 1, 2024.

5. Rebecca Joy Norlander et al., *Entrepreneurship: Where Urban Libraries Fit* (New York: Knology, April 30, 2022), https: //www.urbanlibraries.org/files/White-Paper_Libraries-as -Ent-Hubs_2022-04-26.pdf.

6. "Transcript: Tressie McMillan Cottom Interviews Emily Drabinski," *The Ezra Klein Show / New York Times*, September 2023, https://www.nytimes.com/2023/09/12 /podcasts/transcript-tressie-mcmillan-cottom-interviews -emily-drabinski.html.

Afterword

1. https://civiccommons.us/2018/01/measuring-civic-commons/.
2. https://civiccommons.us/2019/01/measure-matters-diy -toolkit/.
3. Richard V. Reeves and Coura Fall, "Seven Key Takeaways from Chetty's New Research on Friendship and Economic Mobility," Brookings Institution, August 2, 2022, https://www .brookings.edu/articles/7-key-takeaways-from-chettys -new-research-on-friendship-and-economic-mobility/.
4. Andre M. Perry, Jonathan Rothwell, and David Harshbarger, "The Devaluation of Assets in Black Neighborhoods," November 27, 2018, Brookings Institution, https://www.brookings .edu/articles/devaluation-of-assets-in-black-neighborhoods/.
5. Andre M. Perry and Hannah Stephens, "Investment Without Displacement: How a Surge of Development Changed— and Didn't Change—One Detroit Neighborhood," January 24, 2024, https://www.brookings.edu/articles/investment -without-displacement-how-a-surge-of-development -changed-and-didnt-change-one-detroit-neighborhood/.
6. Ibid.